Olivier Lagalisse

HOW TO MAKE AN OLD DOG HAPPY

Preface by Dr Fabienne Aujard

*Translated from the French and adapted
by Elfreda Powell*

Souvenir Press
London

First published in Great Britain 2005 by Souvenir Press
43 Great Russell St London WC1B 3PD

First published in France 2004 by Editions Le Cherche-Midi
under the title of *J'aide mon chien à bien vieillir*

English translation © copyright 2005 Souvenir Press and Elfreda Powell

The right of Olivier Lagalisse to be identified as author of this work has
been asserted by him in accordance with the Copyright, Designs and
Patents Act 1988.

ISBN 0 28563 733 9

Typeset by FiSH Books
Printed and bound by Cambridge University Press

To
Toupie, Moustique, Taupe, Tarzan,
Maya, Socrates, Kebab, Youki,
Lisa, Gus, Sherlock
and
Figaro
who,
I am sure,
are waiting for me somewhere...
O.L.

Acknowledgements

The author would like to thank the many people who helped him to complete this project, and in particular: Léa Naty, Véronique Grillon, Fabienne Aujard, Claudine Colozzi, Corinne Liger-Marie, Ivan Ballini, Olivier Leynaud, the Town Hall of Asnières-sur-Seine, not to mention the technical advice of Barney of Green Ireland and Heming of La Radaserie.

The translator would like to thank Simon Felger Bvet Med MRCV for reading the English text and for his helpful comments.

Contents

Short glossary of the most common pathologies found in elderly dogs

When a dog grows old...

There was once a dog who, when faced with a wild animal, had always been full of courage and swift in its pursuit, and had always pleased his master, but under the heavy weight of his years he began to lose his prowess.

One day, when he came face to face with a badly wounded wild boar, he seized it by the ear, to do battle, but because of his bad teeth, he had to let his prey go and he stood there with his mouth agape.

The unhappy hunter rebuked his dog, but the old dog replied laconically: 'It's not my courage that has let you down, but my strength. You praise what I was in the past, but condemn what I am now.'

Well, Philetus, you can see all too clearly my motive for writing this fable.

PHAEDRUS, *Fables*

Preface

by Dr Fabienne Aujard

As far as we know not a single living thing is spared the phenomenon of growing old. Consequently, growing old well is something that preoccupies all of us. So it will hardly come as a surprise that we also worry about our faithful companions' well-being in their old age.

Research on aging, or gerontology, is one of the disciplines which has shown great scientific advances over the last two decades. There is a growing awareness of the physical and mental conditions necessary to maintain an optimal quality of life in elderly people. And, thanks to a better knowledge of the aging process, prospects of a longer life for man can only increase – a fact we owe to a better understanding of our needs, whether psychological or social. For example, having a sensible attitude towards nutrition from an early age not only lengthens life expectancy, but helps one to keep fit to an advanced age. Psychological comfort is particularly important in maintaining elderly people's well-being, and a considerable effort is now taking place to maintain a socially rich environment and various kinds of mental stimulation for old people.

Companion animals have also benefited from scientific advances in gerontology, and as a result over the years the life prospect for dogs of all breeds has increased. Whether it is in the field of veterinary care, hygiene and nutrition, or knowledge of canine behaviour, a better respect for the dog is reflected in people's attitudes.

Because dogs are now living longer, a more and more significant part of a vet's clientele is made up of elderly dogs. The market in drugs has adapted to the growing demand by owners of 'senior' dogs, and it is now possible for the owner to respond to the needs of his companion throughout his life, thanks to the ranges of foods and vitamin supplements that have been specially adapted to old age.

Because the phenomenon of aging is not an identical process from one animal to the next and it is not always easy to make sense of it, a guide like *How to Make an Old Dog Happy* was very necessary. As a canine behaviourist and author of an earlier guide to the history of different breeds, *The Company of Dogs* (not yet available in English), Olivier Lagalisse once again gives us an opportunity to profit from his experience and his passion for dogs. He begins with a clear, accessible presentation of all the main signs of aging and the most common illnesses encountered in old dogs, and alerts you, the owners, to all the different features that you must not neglect as you prepare your dog for old age. Any owner who cares for his or her companion's well-being will find here simple recipes and shrewd advice that can easily be adopted in everyday life. As for caring, this also means anticipating, and the advice given in this guide should be applied from a very early age when looking after your dog.

There are few books devoted to the elderly dog, and *How to Make an Old Dog Happy* is a comprehensive guide, for all the different fields associated with aging are treated here in detail: What veterinary treatments are adapted to elderly dogs? How do you maintain the physical condition (both external and internal) of your animal over the years? How do you adapt your behaviour and that of your nearest and dearest to the particular needs of aging dogs? How to you stimulate your dog's mental functioning and help it keep its will to live? And finally to what organisations can you turn to accompany your dog to the end of his life?

Through his broad understanding of dogs, Olivier Lagalisse provides useful and practical elements which will help you to take charge of your elderly animal. Every owner wishes a long and peaceful life for his or her dog, and you will find the answers to your questions here. This is a guide you can turn to from day to day to discover the simple things you can do to give your faithful companion the comfortable and happy old age that it deserves.

(Dr Aujard is a specialist in aging and a qualified vet, a Doctor in Sciences and a researcher for the Centre National de la Recherche Scientifique – The National Centre for Scientific Research)

Introduction

While dogs grow old just like any other living creature, with the formidable progress that has taken place in the last twenty years or so in the fields of selection, hygiene, nutrition and behavioural studies, we can now talk of a third, even a fourth age for dogs. In France, for example, 56 per cent of dogs currently reach an age of twelve years, and nearly 12 per cent pass the sixteen mark. So, though 'senior', man's best friend can still look forward to many more adventures to be lived out at its master's side, as long as its owner can compensate for the inevitable decline of his or her faithful companion's physical and intellectual capacities with psychological understanding and love.

Any animal that is dependent on man has the right to proper sustenance and care.

It must, under no circumstances, be abandoned or killed unjustifiably.

Article 5 of the Universal Declaration of Animal Rights, proclaimed by Unesco in Paris on 15 October 1978.

Every domestic animal that man has chosen as a companion has the right to a comfortable life span, and to its natural old age, and its owner must ensure that everything within his power is done to achieve this.

Article 6, *Ibid.*

Aging: all dogs are not equal

Every man desires to live long; but no man would be old

JONATHAN SWIFT

Between the minuscule mayfly which lives but a few hours and the giant tortoise, whose 200 years is a record for vertebrates' longevity, in the animal kingdom the dog is classified in the lower range of life expectancy.

ANIMAL	AVERAGE LIFESPAN	RECORD LONGEVITY
Canary	12-15 years	34 years
Cat	13-17 years	36 years
Chimpanzee	25-35 years	55 years
Cow	9-12 years	25 years
Dog	9-15 years	29 years
Elephant	30-35 years	84 years
Fox	8-10 years	15 years
Guinea pig	3-4 years	14 years
Horse	20-25 years	62 years
Parrot	35-40 years	70 years
Rabbit	6-8 years	15 years
Rat	3-4 years	7 years
Sheep	10-12 years	25 years
Trout	25-30 years	44 years
Wolf	10-12 years	17 years

Ancestors of the dog, wolves (*Canis lupus*) on average live for around twelve years in the wild and fifteen to sixteen years in captivity (Wolf Park at Chabrières)

In the case of carnivores, among the thirty-five species that make up the family of Canidae, and that include the dingo, jackal, coyote, fox and of course wolf (ancestor of all dogs), the canine species appears to enjoy the longest life-span, the causes of natural death – rigours of climate, predators, accidents as well as certain infectious diseases such as rabies – having normally been eliminated through domestication. However, we must somewhat modify this claim, as the potential life-span of a dog varies considerably from one breed to another. Generally speaking, small and medium sized dogs are reputed to live longer than their fellow creatures which belong to the more imposing breeds.

AVERAGE LIFE EXPECTANCY OF DIFFERENT DOG BREEDS

SMALL BREEDS

Bichon frise	13 years	Chihuahua	16 years	Pekingese	14 years
Border terrier	15 years	Coton de Tuléar	17 years	Scottish terrier	15 years
Cairn terrier	17 years	Tibetan spaniel	15 years	Miniature spitz	16 years
Toy poodle	16 years	Toy spaniel	17 years	Dachshund	14 years
Pug	14 years	Jack Russell	15 years	Welsh corgi	16 years
Cavalier King Charles spaniel	15 years	Lhasa Apso	15 years	Yorkshire terrier	16 years

MEDIUM SIZE BREEDS

American Staffordshire terrier	13 years	Bull terrier	13 years	Irish terrier	15 years
Basset hound	13 years	Miniature poodle	19 years	German Pinscher	17 years
Beagle	14 years	Chow-chow	13 years	Schapendoes (Dutch sheepdog)	15 years
Pyrenean mountain dog	14 years	Cocker spaniel	14 years	Standard Schnauzer	14 years
French bulldog	13 years	Brittany spaniel	14 years	Shar Pei	13 years
English bulldog	11 years	Fox terrier	15 years	Whippet	16 years

LARGE BREEDS

Airedale terrier	13 years	Cane Corso	12 years	Golden Retriever	12 years
Alsatian	12 years	Collie	13 years	Husky	13 years
Berger de Beauce	13 years	Dalmatian	13 years	Labrador	12 years
Berger de Brie (Briard)	12 years	Dobermann	12 years	German shepherd	13 years
Weimaraner	12 years	Dogo Canario	12 years	Pointer	13 years
Boxer	11 years	Dogo Argentino	12 years	Irish setter	13 years

VERY LARGE DOGS

Anatolian shepherd dog	10 years	Tibetan mastiff	10 years	Mastiff	9 years
Bernese mountain dog	10 years	Fila Brasilero	10 years	Neapolitan mastiff	9 years
Bull mastiff	10 years	Greyhound	10 years	Spanish mastiff	9 years
Deerhound	11 years	Irish wolfhound	10 years	Pyrenean mountain dog	10 years
German mastiff	8 years	Landseer	9 years	Saint Bernard	9 years
Dogue de Bordeaux (French mastiff)	9 years	Leonberger	10 years	Newfoundland	8 years

Yorkshire terrier

Beagle

Berger de Brie (Briard)

Neapolitan mastiff

Nicknamed, respectively, the Apollo of dogs and the Saint Bernard of the Seas, the German mastiff and the Newfoundland have, alas, two of the shortest life expectancies in the canine world

Once you know your dog's life expectancy, you, as a responsible owner, can foresee the time when your dog will enter the third age and so be able to make the necessary preparations for it. So:

- A miniature breed of dog will become 'senior' at around ten years old
- A medium-size breed of dog will become 'senior' at about eight years old
- A large breed of dog will become 'senior' at about seven years old
- A very large breed of dog will become 'senior' at around five years old.

The above rules are not hard and fast and there are many exceptions to them. Certain dogs, although belonging to small breeds, do not, in fact, live for all that long: take, for example, the case of the English bulldog, which although comparable in height to the miniature poodle has barely half that dog's life expectancy. In contrast, some lines of giant breeds that have been competently and carefully selected by conscientious breeders who are anxious to improve these companion dogs' welfare, have seen their life expectancy grow: some German bulldogs, deerhounds and Irish wolfhounds can also reach the venerable age of thirteen. (While on this subject, it would be a wise move, when you purchase a puppy, to find out more about the lifespan of its line, rather than allow yourself to be beguiled by the so-called titles that champions are sometimes given.)

And what about the delightful mongrel (a dog that has been produced by parents which are not pedigree)? The numerous blood lines to be found in their genetic ancestry (which limits the appearance of hereditary diseases linked to consanguinity) as well as the

pitiless selection to which they have been subjected (the elimination of the weakest or the least resourceful) appear to give them a slight edge over their fellow dogs, as far as life expectancy goes. It must be said too that in the longevity stakes mongrels with a small build outstrip their bigger counterparts.

Contrary to what happens in the human race, where females outlive males, gender does not appear to be a determining factor in the life expectancy of the canine species.

Just like Siska (at three months), mongrels have a tendency to revert to their 'wild' colour: fawn and grey, and to an average build of around 50 cm to the withers. They represent 65 per cent of the French canine population

Factors of aging

Patou, the old guard dog, said:
'You know, I was young once…
I had my youthful bloom,
A passionate eye, a heart on fire'

EDMOND ROSTAND – *Chantecler*

With the dog, just as with all other animals, senescence, or biological aging, is due to the progressive deterioration of almost all the organism's functions. In fact, through time, cells gradually stop renewing themselves, blood vessels lose their elasticity and clog up while the different organs show a certain wear and tear (the formation of free radicals and glycosylative reactions). This degeneration, as well as the decreasing performance resulting from this, varies considerably from one individual to another, for there are several factors that can lead to premature aging.

⊕ **Heredity:** This is the principal factor, the influence of which is indisputable. Each dog's genetic inheritance, directly inherited from its parents, determines 'on paper' its life expectancy. A dog which comes from a healthy, vigorous line whose members have lived to an advanced age has every chance of reproducing the same type.

⊕ **Obesity:** This is the great enemy of longevity in dogs, as it accelerates the aging process by aggravating cardiac and respiratory problems, not to mention the deterioration of bones and joints. Although certain breeds like the Basset hound, Cocker spaniel and Brittany spaniel, Labrador, Dachshund and West Highland White terrier seem more predisposed to obesity than others like the Greyhound, Whippet or Fox terrier, being overweight affects one in two dogs. The age and sex of the dog have a direct bearing on its possible obesity: 32 per cent of females are affected by it as opposed to an average of 23 per cent of males.

Contrary to appearances, Marcy, a seven-year-old Rottweiler bitch, is not expecting a happy event: she is 25 kilograms overweight!

PERCENTAGE OF OBESE DOGS ACCORDING TO AGE AND SEX
(after Mason)

DOG'S AGE	MALE	FEMALE
1-4 years	12 %	21%
5-7 years	30%	37%
8-11 years	34%	41%
More than 12 years	41%	40%

⊕ **Stress:** Unfortunately this is rarely taken into account by animal owners, and is often due to the loss of territorial markers at the time of a change in environment or too frequent changes of abode (car, train, aeroplane). Every weekend, all over the world, dogs take part in shows and competitions, and whatever they are, they are more subject than others to anxiety crises, hypertension, eczema, asthma and digestive pathologies. There is no doubt that certain owners' 'championitis' will accelerate their 'champion's' aging process in this way.

⊕ **Sport:** While this may be indispensable in encouraging a good physical and psychological balance in your dog, primarily by developing its breathing, quick wittedness and musculature, it must, first and foremost, be a pleasure, and remain a recreational activity for the animal. Practised in too intensive a manner or to an advanced age, Ringcraft, Canicross, Agility, Chasing a decoy, Coursing, track racing, sled races, obstacle jumps can become a veritable calvary for the dog, and besides being the cause of numerous heart attacks, can lead to serious lesions of muscles, bones and joints. Overexploited by totally irresponsible owners, certain Hound breeds, like the Greyhound, Whippet, Galgo, Afghan, Azawakh, Magyar Agar, and Saluki can become completely worn out by the time they are three years old.

⊕ **Reproduction:** While this obviously allows the breeder to perpetuate the breed and produce new generations, it can also have disastrous consequences when it is practised too frequently, the stress and fatigue of the male dog performing many hundreds of matings a year is nothing in comparison to the apathy and exhaustion (anaemia, lack of calcium) of the poor bitches used for breeding, which sometimes have to endure two litters every year throughout their life, since there is no menopause in Canidae.

In order to prevent the possible appearance of mammary tumours or other cysts and above all to prevent the birth of abnormal puppies, a bitch more than seven years old should no longer be allowed to breed.

⊕ **Lack of care and attention:** While preventative veterinary care is available in terms of vaccines, various treatments, annual check-ups etc., nutrition (quality foods adapted for every age and situation), or more simply, common upkeep (brushing, bathing, physical and play activities, regular walks), the attention that a dog's master or mistress gives to his or her dog will be the determining factor in that dog's lifespan: a dog that ages well is first and foremost a dog which has a will to live.

The Retired Greyhound Trust (tel: 0208335 3016) was set up in 1976 to give old greyhounds a new and happier life and since then has looked after over 31,000: 3,100 in 2004 alone. They do not have their own kennels but rehome the dogs or hire space in kennels all over the country and at the time of going to press are paying for 460 greyhounds to be kennelled. Learn more about them on www.retiredgreyhounds.co.uk

Signs of growing old

Some bitches can live for up to twenty years.
So it is thought that the poet Homer was telling the truth when he said
that Argos, Ulysses' dog, died when he was twenty years old.

ARISTOTLE, *History of Animals*

Although there are many signs of aging, which often manifest them-selves in an insidious way, they are not always easy to detect. Through an early diagnosis, however, you can prevent too rapid a decline in your dog's physical and mental faculties. Some simple observations and a bit of logic will set any owner who is in touch with his dog on the right path.

CORRESPONDENCE BETWEEN HUMAN AND CANINE AGES
Table of equivalents

DOG'S AGE	Small breeds	Medium size breeds	Large breeds	Very large breeds
6 months	15 years	12 years	10 years	8 years
1 year	20 years	18 years	12 years	14 years
18 months	24 years	21 years	16 years	18 years
2 years	28 years	27 years	25 years	22 years
3 years	32 years	33 years	30 years	31 years
4 years	36 years	39 years	37 years	40 years
5 years	40 years	45 years	48 years	50 years
6 years	44 years	51 years	58 years	60 years
7 years	48 years	57 years	65 years	68 years
8 years	52 years	63 years	72 years	77 years
9 years	56 years	69 years	80 years	86 years
10 years	60 years	75 years	88 years	94 years
11 years	64 years	80 years	96 years	105 years
12 years	68 years	85 years	105 years	120 years
13 years	72 years	90 years	112 years	
14 years	76 years	95 years	120 years	
15 years	80 years	102 years		
16 years	84 years	110 years		
17 years	88 years	120 years		
18 years	94 years			
19 years	100 years			
20 years	110 years			
	HUMAN AGE			

By comparing the real age of your animal with its human 'equivalent', you will already get a better idea of what shape your dog is in and how much energy and drive it still has. If you bear in mind that a human becomes 'senior' once he has passed the halfway mark in his life expectancy, at around 50-55, you will see that you should be particularly attentive towards your dog once it reaches the age of six to eight years old, depending on its size and breed.

Milord, 17 years old — the equivalent of 100 years old in human terms

The first signs to be on the alert for are morphological ones. The silhouette of your dog is gradually and progressively going to change, after which more subtle changes will begin to appear.

⊕ **Weakening of the muscles:** This condition is connected with fewer physical activities. At the same time, the dog's neck becomes stronger and its head begins to look more angular.

⊕ **Obesity** will occur as a result of the dog reducing its efforts and moving around less, but it is primarily a sign of its metabolism slowing down: the dog is no longer getting rid of his daily food intake which is too rich.

⊕ **Getting thin** is a sign of troubles in the digestive system, of a loss of appetite or more simply that teeth and gums are so painful that the dog is taking in the least possible food in order to avoid the discomfort of eating it.

⊕ **The line of the back** is gradually becoming hollow, or perhaps the opposite, arching, and the dog has a less mobile bottom (which all point to difficulties in moving), front paws are spreading, the dog is carrying its head down or towards one side or the other: all these indicate the inevitable onslaught of old age on the skeleton (arthritis, for example).

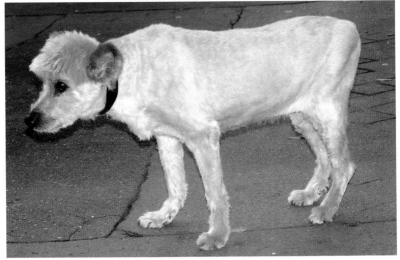

A hollow line of the back, head held low and a significant weakening of the muscles for Daisy, a small, 16-year-old female Pyrenean mountain dog

Just like humans, dogs go grey. Going grey varies according to the breed: towards 5-6 years old for the biggest dogs as opposed to 10-12 for the smallest

⊕ **The coat** becomes lifeless and brittle. Once it has lost its vitality, hair falls out in patches, with no relation to the usual moulting periods. The skin thickens and loses its elasticity.

⊕ **Going grey** White hair begins to appear, first around the muzzle, then the eyes. This phenomenon will over time end up covering the whole of the dog's face.

SIGNS OF GROWING OLD

Biological constants

The aging of the organs brings about an important modification in their functioning. Understanding the physiology of your elderly dog will be greatly facilitated if you compare it with a younger animal's. Anything that departs from the normal biological constants should be interpreted as an invitation to consult a vet.

⊕ **Temperature** 38.5 degrees C (slightly lower for certain breeds like the Husky)

⊕ **Pulse rate** **The younger a dog is, the quicker its heart beat.**
- Puppy   = about 120 beats a minute
- Adult   = about 100 beats
- Elderly dog = about 80 beats

The bigger a dog is, the slower its heart beat.
- *Saint Bernard, German bulldog* = 70 beats a minute
- *Poodle, Brittany spaniel*   = 90 beats a minute
- *Miniature spitz, Yorkshire terrier* = 120 beats a minute

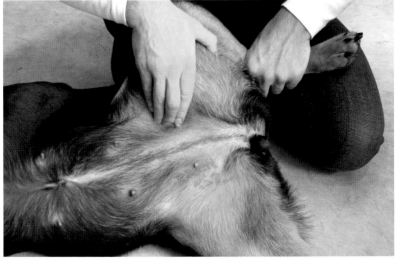

You absolutely must wait until the dog is relaxed for at least ten minutes before measuring its pulse

In order to measure your animal's pulse correctly, your dog must be calm and relaxed. The best place to feel the blood flow is the femoral artery, which is easy to locate on the inside of the top of the thigh when the dog is lying on its side (the femoral hollow). After placing two fingertips on the artery, you count the number of beats for one minute (if the dog cannot keep still, just count the beats for fifteen seconds and then multiply the result by four to obtain the pulse rate).

⊕ **Breathing:** Breathing is normal if there are between 15 and 30 intakes a minute. It will vary with stress, size and the animal's stoutness.

⊕ **Blood:** Blood represents 7.2 per cent of the animal's weight (80-90 ml of blood per kilogram of live weight). It is composed of:

red corpuscles
* Haemoglobin: 12-18 g/100ml
* Erythrocytes: 5.5-8.5 millions/ml
* Haematocrit: 37-55 per cent

white corpuscles
* Leucocytes: 6-18 per cent
* Neutrophils (or polymorphs): 60-77 per cent
* Lymphocytes: 12-30 per cent
* Monocytes: 3-10 per cent
* Eosinophils: 2-10 per cent
* Basophils: 0.

Bleeding time: 2-3 minutes
Coagulation time: 6-8 minutes

There are eight main types of canine blood groups. If a dog needs a transfusion, it can receive practically any type of blood so long as it is its very first blood transfusion. For a second transfusion, it is absolutely essential that it receive blood coming from the same blood group as its own.

⊕ **Urine:** Depending on body size, a dog evacuates 0.5 to 2 litres of urine a day, of a pH of between 5.5 and 7, and a density of 1,016-1,060.

Chemical components:

- Glucose: 70-100 mg/100ml
- Calcium: 9-11 mg/100ml
- Phosphorus: 2.2-4 mg/100ml
- Blood urea: 17-28 mg/100 ml
- Creatinine: 1-1.7 mg/100 ml

The appearance of certain physiological phenomena associated with aging shows that the animal is already suffering from its effects. It is essential that your animal is examined as soon as possible to see how far the pathology has progressed.

⊕ **Cough, or panting** can sometimes be indicators of pulmonary or cardiac problems (such as oedema).

⊕ **Increase in thirst and urination** often comes from malfunctioning kidneys, diabetes or Cushing's disease.

You can very quickly check whether your elderly dog is dehydrated or not. Simply pinch between thumb and index finger a bit of its skin just above the shoulder at the level of the withers, and gently twist it. If, as soon as you release it, the skin immediately returns to normal, then the individual is well hydrated (a supple and elastic skin). If on the other hand where you pinched the skin, it remains visibly raised for several seconds, the dog is dehydrated: you need to see a vet urgently as dehydration can be a revealing sign of a much more serious internal problem.

⊕ **Difficulty in urinating:** can come from cystitis, from a prostate infection, from bladder stones, or from a tumour.

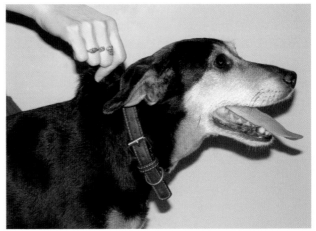

A simple little tweak before Tipoune goes for a walk tells her owner of her state of hydration. Tipoune is an eleven-year-old, female, fox terrier cross

⊕ **A distended abdomen:** when there is a cardiac insufficiency on the right side, the liver becomes engorged with blood, which then causes an accumulation of plasma in the abdominal cavity (ascites).

⊕ **Lumps on the body or limbs:** these tumours are not necessarily malignant.

⊕ **A milky veil over the eye:** known as a 'cataract', the crystalline lens of the eye gradually becomes opaque and ultimately the dog will lose its sight in that eye.

⊕ **Yellow or brownish teeth:** coupled with fetid breath indicate the presence of tartar, which, unless removed, can jeopardise the health of the dog's teeth and gums.

Mental problems

Just like all its other organs, a dog's brain ages. This aging of the brain, which is for the most part a result of a less efficient flow of blood, provokes a psychomotor slow-down, which in turn can lead to numerous behavioural problems.

⊕ **Cognitive problems:** These relate to the treatment of information and to learning mechanisms. The dog has difficulty in getting its bearings in space. Sometimes it seems to be wandering aimlessly, becomes dirty and does not respond to its name. It no longer respects social rules or established hierarchies, and the animal can become aggressive towards other dogs and then towards humans (lacking its usual inhibition about biting).

⊕ **Emotional problems:** The dog has anxiety crises. It can develop a 'paroxysmal digestive' anxiety (hypersalivation, vomiting) or a permanent anxiety which is translated into 'substitutive' licking, which in turn can lead to lesions, notably on its paws or tail.

⊕ **Mood swings (problems relating to the thymus gland):** The dog shows unstable and unpredictable behaviour, passing suddenly from a state of indolence to hyperactivity; this brusque change of attitude can be provoked at any moment by any random stimulus: the fall of a leaf, a banging door, switching a light off or on etc. As in human psychiatry, these sudden changes of mood reflect the development of quite serious depression.

Substitutive licking must be interpreted as an alarm bell, for it reveals emotional problems that are sometimes brought on by boredom or inactivity

An old dog's most common ailments

My poor old Julio is still alive. He's given enemas of wine and beef stock and now he is going to be given vesicatories [blistering agents]. The vet won't be surprised now if he passes away.

The day before yesterday, his feet were cold, and we looked at him, thinking that he was going to die. He's exactly like a person – he makes those little gestures that are so deeply human.

GUSTAVE FLAUBERT – Letter to his niece Caroline, 1879

Obviously, this chapter is no substitute for a consultation with a vet, but it will help you, the lay owner, to detect and understand the process of the most common pathologies that can affect your old companion. This summary of knowledge will then help you to avoid the pitfalls of a 'do-it-yourself diagnosis', which in turn may lead to 'I thought I was doing the right thing', or self-medication, always a bad thing for an animal and very difficult for the professional to put right afterwards.

⊕ **Heart problems:** With age, the cardiac chambers become slack, the valves which control the passage of blood between the auricles and ventricles can start leaking, and as a result cardiac murmurs start occurring as well as a weakening of the myocardium (heart muscle) which, now tired, pumps out less blood towards the blood vessels.

• **A cardiac insufficiency of the right side** means that the liver becomes engorged with blood: the plasma which then accumulates in the abdominal cavity will distend the dog's abdomen (ascites).

• **A cardiac insufficiency on the left side** leads to the retention of reoxygenated blood in the lungs, in the pulmonary alveoli, which in turn leads to the appearance of an oedema, causing a cough and respiratory difficulties (panting).

X-rays, electrocardiogram and echo scan will help the vet to prescribe specific medicines to sustain the heart. A diet low in sodium (salt) will sometimes be recommended.

⊕ **Kidney problems:** Problems of the kidney, which is without any doubt the dog's most fragile organ, are the second most common cause of death among elderly dogs. The progressive loss of the kidneys' capacity to filter waste from the body brings about the accumulation of numerous toxins in the blood, causing serious lesions like ulcers or demineralisation of the bones.

From the amounts of urea and creatinine, it will be easy to diagnose whether there is a kidney problem. The treatment of the disease will facilitate the elimination of waste and will be reinforced by an appropriate diet (best quality proteins, little or no phosphorus, more vitamins and energy-giving supplements).

⊕ **Liver diseases:** As with the kidneys, the liver has a detoxifying function. The secretion of bile helps the organism to transform sugars and proteins. Liver insufficiency in an old dog is often the consequence of inflammation and infections, but can also equally occur as a result of prolonged medical treatments or doses of medicine given in the wrong proportions. Loss of weight and appetite are, along with vomiting, the first symptoms of hepatitis; diarrhoea and the appearance of jaundice (icterus) merely confirm the diagnosis at a more advanced stage. After a blood test and a hepatic biopsy, a diet without any salt and low in proteins will most certainly be prescribed.

⊕ **Arthritis:** This degenerative disease which generally affects dogs of more than seven years old (old-age arthritis) is characterised by a progressive destruction of the cartilage of the joints, which is associated with the formation of osteophytes (extra bone). It can be due to malformations of the bones (Hip dysplasia), to badly repaired fractures, to dislocations, to too much exercise (with sporting dogs) or, in the case of fat animals, to being overweight. The dog drags its paw, finds it difficult to stand up, or to climb steps; these symptoms have a

When there is inflammation in the joints (arthritis), a gentle circular massage of the painful regions (knees, hips, elbows, shoulders) will help eliminate the toxins that have accumulated and are causing the pain.

tendency to become less marked when the dog has warmed up. Over time the arthritis will become chronic and debilitating; at times when the pain is very intense, the animal can become aggressive if touched.

While anti-inflammatories are the traditional treatment for arthritis, quite recently medications have come on the market which contain substances (glucosamine and chondroitin sulphate) that can spread as far as the cartilage and stabilise the development of lesions in the bone joints.

A short regular massage, using the fingertips and lasting about ten minutes every day will relax the stiff muscles and joints, while stimulating circulation of the blood. In small breeds, a warm bath from time to time will temporarily give a bit of suppleness to painful joints.

⊕ **Obesity:** While this may not be thought of as a proper illness, it is an aggravating factor in all the pathologies of the elderly dog. It predisposes him or her to cardiovascular diseases, osteoarthritis, kidney disease and also diabetes. Excess weight considerably diminishes the life expectancy of an animal. A progressive resumption of exercise means that the dog will avoid becoming stiff. Putting the dog on a diet or specific dietary food is imperative if you want your dog to return to well being.

⊕ **Eye diseases:** In an elderly dog, these are mainly degeneration of the retina and cataract. These pathologies can present themselves singly or together.

• **Degeneration of the retina:** Often hereditary, particularly in the Berger de Brie (Briard), poodle, collie, English setter, Gordon setter, Irish setter, it can also result from poisoning, tumours or nutritionally deficient food. Due to a fault in the structure of the retina at the time of its embryonic development or to progressive degeneration of a normal retina, it manifests itself as irremediable loss of sight ending in blindness. The evolution of disease will be monitored by examining the back of the eye, an angiograph or an electro-retino-gram.

• **Cataract:** When the crystalline lens of the eye becomes opaque, it prevents light rays from reaching the retina, and gradually plunges the animal into blindness. The Alsatian, poodle, Water spaniel, Bobtail, Golden retriever and Labrador are among the most vulnerable breeds. The cataract which manifests itself as a characteristic whitening of the pupil, generally appears in dogs of more than eight

years old. When the retina is in good condition, surgical intervention remains the best treatment.

Degeneration of the retina and cataract have made Tequila, a twelve-year-old Labrador, totally blind.

⊕ **Oral and dental diseases:** These occur very frequently in old dogs (75 per cent of animals of more than ten years old have dental problems), and the loss of teeth and gum infections can hurt the dog when it chews, so that sometimes the dog will refuse to eat. A cause of bad breath, the accumulation of tartar predisposes the dog to cardiac and renal diseases. Although necessary, the removal of tartar by ultrasound is to be used with caution for it requires a general anaesthetic – this is always a delicate situation when it comes to very elderly subjects. Good oral and dental hygiene (brushing, chewable dentifrice, dental gel) will help to space out treatments (which should be every two years).

⊕ **Mammary tumours:** One bitch in two develops mammary tumours between the ages of nine and twelve. Very frequently, these take the form of small 'coffee beans' (nodules) in the mammary tissue, and then rapidly increase in size and volume. They are referred to as 'benign' when the nodules remain localised and show no risk of spreading, and as 'malignant' when the affected cells are cancerous and multiply rapidly. Only a histological analysis of the tumour tissue can tell us what sort of tumour has developed. In the case of benign tumours, the prognosis is extremely favourable; in the case of malignant tumours it is much more doubtful. The treatment is in all cases surgical and must be done at the earliest possible moment: the survival rate of two years after the removal of a tumour less than 5 cms across is 70 per cent, whereas it is only 20 per cent when the tumour is greater than 10 cm in diameter.

Happily for Gitane, a fourteen-year-old poodle bitch, her mammary tumours, though large, are benign

⊕ **Cancer:** The lengthening of a dog's lifespan has naturally brought with it an increase in the number of cases of cancer, since the risk of cancer increases with age. But while more and more elderly dogs are faced with the disease, the formidable progress realised in human medicine has for the most part been adapted into veterinary medicine, and so there is a much more favourable prognosis. Tomographic (tomodensitometric) examination (by a scanner) is also now used in addition to classic radiography, while chemotherapy and radiotherapy have become common in fighting against the development of metastases. Let us not forget that certain types of cancer, such as lymphoma, can be cured in a greater and greater number of cases.

⊕ **Degenerative depression** This behavioural problem is very frequently found in elderly dogs. Bitches from eight years old onwards seem to be more prone to it than male dogs (39 per cent as against 20 per cent). The symptoms of this depression are also very upsetting for the owner: the dog isolates herself, avoids contact with the rest of the group (the family), does not respond to orders, becomes deaf when one mentions her name, sleeps very little, wanders about aimlessly, dragging her paws, does her business anywhere, and licks herself constantly. Equally, she can also begin to ingest non-digestible substances (a condition known as pica), like pebbles or earth, as well as licking the ground, walls and sometimes even trees in a chronic manner. This degenerative depression often begins after a more or less long hyper-attachment, during which the dog cannot bear to be away from her master. The medical treatment prescribed by the vet must be linked very closely to a proper re-education in behaviour (often several months long) and carried out with patience and gentleness so that the animal can gradually emerge from its isolation, find its bearings and its *joie de vivre* again by remaking contact with the group: in certain scientific details, canine degenerative depression is very comparable to Alzheimer's in humans.

🐕 **It is absolutely essential that you do not isolate the dog, for, even if it does not move around much, shutting it away in a room** under the pretext that it can rest there better or that it will be easier to clean the floor afterwards (as opposed to the carpet in the sitting-room) will end up completely excluding the poor animal from the world at large and so aggravate its depression irretrievably.

⊕ **Confusional syndrome** For a long time this has been confused with degenerative depression. It can be distinguished however by the fact that the dog presents only cognitive problems, its moods and emotions are not an issue. This cognitive disorganisation, other than problems caused by loss of learning (and therefore of cleanliness), is manifested in problems connected with:

• **bearings:** the animal can get lost on a route that it has taken every day for as long as ten years;

• **assessment of space and volume**: the dog, for example, tries to get inside a shoe-box when he has the size of a Saint Bernard;

• **loss of a sense of time:** the animal starts to sleep more and more in daytime, becoming hyperactive at night.

Eating grass or excrement need not be seen as a sign of psychological problems. The fact that a dog occasionally eats grass until it is sick is often the sign of an inflammation of the mucous in the stomach (gastritis). As for coprophagy (the ingestion of excrement), this is a manifestation of problems of digestive assimilation or a nutritional deficiency: the animal finds in its own stools or in those of other dogs undigested nutrients (starch, fat), which it needs for its own metabolism. It would seem that certain large breeds (Alsatian, Labrador, Irish Wolfhound...), which suffer from a pancreatic insufficiency, are predisposed to coprophagy.

A knowledge, even a very superficial one, of weaknesses and other ailments, presumed to be hereditary, which can affect the breed to which your companion belongs, will help the attentive owner to be forewarned and then to manage these affections better when they appear.

An English bulldog showing possible signs of the beginning of degenerative depression (pica)

A dog which 'grazes' grass often does so to eliminate too full a stomach, through subsequent vomiting.

TABLE OF PRINCIPAL HEREDITARY PREDISPOSITIONS OR WEAKNESSES

MAIN BREEDS	PREDISPOSITIONS
AFGHAN	Necrotising myelopathy (spinal cord degeneration) Certain families are very susceptible to anaesthetics
AIREDALE TERRIER	Umbilical hernias
AKITA INU	Diseases of the retina. Intestinal weaknesses
AMERICAN STAFFORDSHIRE BULL TERRIER	Epilepsy. Frail digestive system. Ataxia cerebellum
BORZOI	Diseases of the retina and optic nerve
BASSET HOUND	Prolapse of the third eyelid. Heart problems
BEAGLE	Cataract. Pulmonary stenosis. Haemophilia A
GERMAN SHEPHERD	Cataract. Aortic stenosis
BELGIAN SHEEPDOG GROENDAEL	Stomach cancer
BELGIAN SHEEPDOG TERVUREN	Epilepsy
BERGER DE BEAUCE	Microphthalmia. Necrotising dermatitis. Hip dysplasia
BERGER DE BRIE (BRIARD)	Retinal atrophy. Hyperthyroid. Urethral ectropion
BERGER DE PICARD	Dysplasia of the photoreceptors
BOBTAIL	Microphthalmia. Weak digestive system
BORDER COLLIE	Behavioural problems (accumulation of lipofuscin). Epilepsy
BORDER TERRIER	Bone disease of the lower jaw
BOSTON TERRIER	Microphthalmia. Renal diabetes insipidus
FRENCH BULLDOG	Entropion. Spinal problems associated with insufficient muscle mass
BOUVIER BERNOIS	Entropion. Coxa-femoral dysplasia
BOUVIER DES FLANDRES	Eczema. Cardio-vascular diseases
GERMAN POINTER	Entropion. Coxa-femoral dysplasia
WEIMARANER	Ectropion. Myotonia. Hernia of the diaphragm.
ENGLISH BULLDOG	Entropion. Pulmonary stenosis (breathing is the breed's weak point)
BULL MASTIFF	Entropion. Degeneration of the cerebellum
BULL TERRIER	Malformation of the eyelids. Deafness
CAIRN TERRIER	Bone disease of the jaws. Eczema. Allergies from fleas. Porto-systemic shunt
CANE CORSO	Entropion. Hip dysplasia
POODLE	Cataract. Diabetes insipidus. Patellar luxation
PUG	Cataract. Ectropion. Loss of balance
CAVALIER KING CHARLES	Microphthalmia. Patellar luxation

As with many breeds that have white coats, certain lines of the Argentine dogo can be predisposed to deafness

CHIHUAHUA	Hydrocephalus. Patellar luxation. Very rapid accumulation of tartar on the teeth
CHOW	Entropion. Ectropion. Eczema
COCKER	Numerous eye infections. Mood swings
COLLIE	Microphthalmia. Odd eye colouration
COTON DE TULEAR	Cardiovascular diseases. Patellar luxation
DALMATIAN	Kidney stones. Deafness
DOBERMANN	Microphthalmia. Cardiomyopathy. Epilepsy. Alopecia
GERMAN MASTIFF	Entropion. Bone diseases. Cardiopathy.
ARGENTINE DOGO	Entropion. Ectropion. Deafness
DOGUE DE BORDEAUX	Entropion. Coxa-femoral dysplasia
TIBETAN MASTIFF	Entropion. Coxa-femoral dysplasia. Eczema
ENGLISH SPRINGER	Numerous eye infections
BRITTANY SPANIEL	Progressive atrophy of the retina. Muscular dystrophy
TOY CONTINENTAL SPANIEL	Entropion. Deafness. Very rapid accumulation of tartar on the teeth
FOX TERRIER	Crystalline lens luxation
GOLDEN RETRIEVER	Progressive retinal atrophy . Hip or elbow dysplasia. Epilepsy
GREYHOUND	Metabolism problems
SIBERIAN HUSKY	Numerous eye infections. Laryngeal paralysis
IRISH WOLFHOUND	Cardiomyopathy. Myelopathy

AN OLD DOG'S MOST COMMON AILMENTS

PARSON RUSSELL TERRIER	Crystalline lens luxation. Patellar luxation. Legg-Calvé-Perthes disease
LABRADOR	Progressive retinal atrophy. Retinal dysphasia. Coxa-femoral dysplasia. Epilepsy
LEONBERGER	Entropion. Hip dysplasia. Joint problems
LHASA APSO	Ectropion. Diabetes insipidus. Renal insufficiency
ALASKAN MALAMUTE	Corneal dystrophy. Joint problems. Haemophilia.
MASTIFF	Microphthalmia. Arthritis
NEAPOLITAN MASTIFF	Inverted eyelids Hip and elbow dysplasia
PYRENEAN MOUNTAIN DOG	Entropion. Cataract. Joint troubles. Eczema
PEKINGESE	Dislocation of the eyeball. Macroglossia. Slipped disc
POINTER	Retinal atrophy. Cataract. Epilepsy. Deafness
RHODESIAN RIDGEBACK	Dermoid sinus (cutaneous malformation which leads to appearance of cysts)
ROTTWEILER	Entropion. Muscular dystrophy. Joint ailments of the elbow and shoulder. Hip dysplasia.
SAINT BERNARD	Entropion. Ectropion. Hip dysplasia. *Genu valgum* (knee bowed inwards) Haemophilia
BLOODHOUND	Entropion. Ectropion.
SAMOYED	Muscular dystrophy. Haemophilia
SCHNAUZER	Microphthalmia. Diabetes insipidus. Dermatoses
SCOTTISH TERRIER	Muscular cramps (Scottish cramps). Eczema
ENGLISH SETTER	Entropion. Behavioural problems (accumulation of lipofuscin)
IRISH SETTER	Microphthalmia. Problems with balance. Allergy to gluten. Haemophilia. Thyroid insufficiency
SHAR-PEI	Numerous eye infections. Amyloidosis. Thyroid insufficiency. Demodectic mange
SPITZ	Eye infections. Dislocation of the shoulder and knee
DACHSHUND	Keratitis. Slipped disc. Very rapid accumulation of tartar on teeth
NEWFOUNDLAND	Ectropion. Aortic stenosis. Kidney stones. Hip dysplasia
TIBETAN TERRIER	Crystalline lens luxation.Behavioural problems (accumulation of lipofuscin)
WELSH CORGI	Cataract. Kidney stones. Hip dysplasia
WEST HIGHLAND WHITE TERRIER	Bone disease of the lower jaw. Legge-Calvé-Perthes disease. Dermatological problems. Very rapid accumulation of tartar on teeth
WHIPPET	Cardiomyopathy. Patellar luxation
YORKSHIRE TERRIER	Microphthalmia. Keratitis. Patellar luxation. Legge-Calvé-Perthes disease. Gingivitis

Preparing your dog
for a happy old age

His hand stroked Aicha's long hair, her moist, panting flanks
'We've got to twelve, my beautiful girl!
We've worked really hard!'
She raised her fine head towards him, her tender eyes, moist with friendship.
He gave her his hands, let her lick them for a moment…

MAURICE GENEVOIX, *Raboliot*

Unlike man, a dog has no awareness of growing old. It is therefore its master's responsibility to help it enter the third age in the same way that he had a duty of care and support while it was growing up. This passage into old age can be done that much more gently if good habits of hygiene are adopted right from the start. The animal should be calm and be used to being handled: its basic behaviours, acquired in youth, will make its master's task much easier when he needs to look after little cuts and sore places, and quite obviously will assist the vet when more serious interventions are necessary.

⊕ **Check ups for elderly dogs:** These are much more elaborate than the simple annual routine visits. These examinations should be carried out from the age of five or six in very large breeds, seven to eight in large breeds, nine to ten in smaller ones. Other than the usual pulse reading, a whole arsenal of impressive complementary tests will be carried out by the vet in order to detect any anomaly: biochemical tests, x-rays, ultrasound scans, urine analysis, blood counts, and a thorough examination of the eyes and ears.

⊕ **Vaccination:** Contrary to what is commonly thought, vaccination is even more necessary in elderly dogs than in young ones, since the immune system in a elderly dog is much less effective. You should agree a vaccination timetable with your vet so that your animal is protected against all the serious viruses. At present, while 80 per cent of all animals of under a year old are correctly protected, only 50 per cent of elderly dogs are.

🐕 Abbreviations for the vaccinations are as follows:
Canine distemper = D; Hepatitis = H; Leptospirosis = L; Parvo virus enteritis = P; Para-influenza = Pi; Rabies = R (for those travelling abroad only).

⊕ **Worming:** Just as with vaccination, worming should be carried out on a very regular basis (between twice and four times a year), even if you don't notice any symptoms. Beware! Not all worming medicines are effective both against round worm (ascari, ancylostoma, trichina) and tapeworm. You should seek advice from your vet. Let me point out that the tapeworm (*Dipylidium caninum*) often develops in a dog after it has been bitten by fleas carrying their larvae or having ingested them when looking for fleas on its own body. Other than symptoms such as diarrhoea or vomiting, the tapeworm often causes irritation of the anal glands. It is therefore of prime importance to treat the animal and its indoor surroundings against fleas first, before worming it.

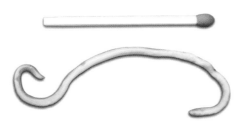

Looking like small strands of spaghetti, roundworms can form a parasitic attachment to a dog simply after he has sniffed the already infected stools of another dog

There is also a parasitic illness, known as Dirofilariosis, which is caused by a worm, the *Dirofilaria immitis*, more commonly known as the 'heart worm'. This disease, which happily is rare in the UK and France (but has spread around the Mediterranean, in Canada, the USA and Mexico) attacks the cardio-vascular system of a dog after it has been contaminated by a mosquito bite, since this insect carries the larvae of this worm. A hundred days after contamination, the larvae invade the pulmonary arteries and are then transported to the right ventricle of the heart, where they spend almost six months developing, after which the females are able to spread microfilaria. As a result of this parasitic invasion, the dog can become very thin and may have difficulties breathing, develop a cough, and a right-sided heart failure...To treat this properly, the adult worms must first be killed, then the microfilaria must be attended to by the vet after the infection has been detected, probably through a blood test, which tests for the presence of antigens of the adult *Dirofilaria* in the animal's blood.

⊕ **Controlling external parasites.** By feeding on the blood of the host dog, fleas, ticks and lice are not only carriers of serious diseases but can also be the cause of numerous allergies.

• **Fleas:** These can easily be identified through the tiny blackish droppings that they leave in the dog's coat, and they can be guaranteed not only to transmit tapeworms but also to provoke very strong allergic reactions. A single flea bite can lead to rashes and itching for up to three weeks.

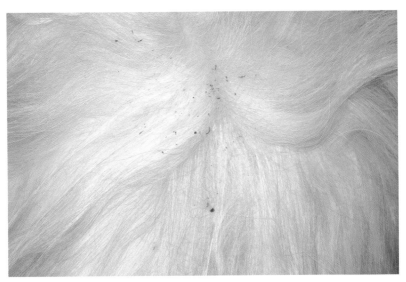

Minute droppings signal the presence of fleas in a Lhasa Apso's long thick coat

🐕 **Both the animal and its indoor surroundings (cushions, bed, basket, carpet etc.) should be treated for parasites since it has been found that fleas never spend more than seven minutes on an animal.**

• **Ticks:** These belong to the acarid family, there are three main species: *Rhipicephalus sanguineus*, *Ixodes ricinus* and *Dermacentor reticulatus*. These parasites feed for two or three days on the dog's blood, and there is a risk that they can transmit diseases such as piroplasmosis and erlichiosis, or borreliosis (Lymé's disease). If you discover a tick attached to your animal's skin (behind the ears, on the flanks, inside the thigh, between its toes…) all you have to do is dislodge the tick by putting a drop of white spirit on it before removing it with a pair of tweezers. Make sure that you remove the head, and thus avoid a cyst forming. The Abbé Godard who was a great expert on Pointers, recommended smearing the tick with a bit of butter or margarine and waiting for it to drop off all by itself.

- **Lice:** Whether it is a question of lice that chew (*Trichodectes canis*) or lice that bite (*Linognathus setosus*), the dog can become infested with them (a condition known as phtiriasis) – white dandruff will appear along with nits that attach themselves to the base of the hair.

- **Anti-parasitic products:** Despite great numbers of them, very few are truly effective. It is best to choose a product that is active for at least a month, resistant to water and to brushing: collars, sprays and pipettes are better than powders (which have often been over-diluted with talcum powder), or shampoos as their effectiveness is dissipated during rinsing), or tablets to be swallowed (which although they may prevent the proliferation of parasites, only work once they have bitten the dog, which means that they are totally useless against allergic reactions to bites), or aerosols (which lose their properties too quickly), or ultrasound apparatus, which, in spite of its high price, has never actually been proved to be effective.

In France, we have several traditional remedies, which are simple, green, yet very effective for getting rid of fleas:
▶ Cover the floor of the kennel or the inside of the basket with cedar wood shavings or leaves from the green walnut tree, or slip them into the dog's cushion.
▶ Cover your hands with peppermint and rub them over the dog (very effective against fleas and ticks).
▶ Make a flea collar by threading eucalyptus seeds on a string and changing it monthly.

Routine daily care

You must not only continue your daily routine of caring, but as your dog grows older, it needs to be intensified. In addition to elementary hygiene and attending to the smallest problems immediately, no matter how trivial they seem (wounds, ticks, fleas, pains), these privileged moments of contact will reassure your animal of its standing in the group, and prevent it from falling into depression by maintaining the points of reference that it has always known; will boost its confidence and the bonds of love that tie it to its master.

⊕ **Brushing** Use a semi-hard brush, and adapt the frequency of your brushing to the animal's coat: once a week for short hair, two or three times a week for long hair. Make sure you get rid of any dirty patches and dead hair (particularly during the moulting season). Brushing will aerate the skin and massage the subcutaneous layer, and therefore also limit skin inflammations and the risk of eczema.

Every fortnight or so, rub the dog down with an old flannel soaked in jojoba oil to bring back the shine and suppleness to a coat that has become dry and brittle, by stimulating the dog's dermis and epidermis.

⊕ **Bathing** Avoid giving very old dogs a bath (there is a risk of them getting cold or of falling). If it is nevertheless imperative for the dog to have a bath, then it should be done very rapidly with a shampoo that is specifically adapted to its coat (human shampoos, even baby ones, are absolutely forbidden). Take particular care to dry the dog properly (with hot towels, hair dryer or rubbing).

Despite all the advertising they get, dry shampoos are not suitable for elderly dogs. Their frequent use will dry out the skin and prevent it from breathing. The trick is to moisten the dog's coat

using a vaporiser (the sort you use to spray indoor plants with), then sprinkling the dog with potato flour before vigorously rubbing it dry for ten minutes or so. Once it has been properly brushed, the coat will be clean, shiny and non-smelly.

⊕ **Cleaning the eyes** This should be done once a week using cottonwool or a paper towel soaked in a normal salt solution, whether it is a camomile concoction or simply water that has been boiled and allowed to cool.

⊕ **Cleaning the ears** This is equally important, particularly if your dog is of a floppy-eared breed. First cut or move away any hair that is blocking the auditory canal, then all you have to do is to put in two or three drops of a specific veterinary product, then gently massage the base of the ear for a minute (to ensure that the product gets to the right spot), before letting your dog eat some grass, so that it can eliminate the impurities in this way.

It is very easy to make your own ear wash by mixing alcohol (70 degrees proof), vinegar and a little water in equal parts: the alcohol will eliminate the bacteria while the vinegar will prevent their reinstatement by acidifying the pH inside the ear. For animals with delicate or sore ears, replace the alcohol and water with sweet almond oil.

⊕ **Cleaning teeth** This should not pose any problem if the dog has been used to it since it was young. If this is not the case, the appearance on the market of toothpaste which has been specially manufactured for dogs makes this task much easier. Let us not forget that 85 per cent of dogs of more than four years of age suffer from **periodontitis**, i.e. an inflammation of the tissues supporting the teeth (the gums) due to tartar and dental plaque.

A simple compress soaked in a solution of bicarbonate of soda then rolled around the finger makes a very suitable 'toothbrush' that is readily accepted by the dog. The good old method of giving the dog a stale crust of bread into which it can sink its teeth two or three times is also very efficient. If the dog accepts it, a raw carrot can be given every three or four

Inflammation of the gums due to the accumulation of tartar (the brown deposit) can rapidly end up loosening the teeth, which may then fall out.

days to crunch and will keep its teeth and gums healthy.

⊕ **Paws** These should be made the subject of particular attention in order to prevent the dog going lame. Having checked that there are no thorns, spikes from plants or small stones lodged in the spaces between the toes, you must carefully cut away the hair growing in the interdigital spaces to prevent it from becoming matted. You must also inspect the pads to look for cracks, worn patches or sores. You should take note that certain 'Nordic' breeds like the Siberian Husky, Alaskan Malamute or Greenland dog have a genetic tendency not to absorb a sufficient amount of zinc. Besides the possibility of hair falling out, this insufficiency can lead to cracked pads. While there are many types of protective shoe or slipper on the market, only those made of **Synpatex** are recommended, because they allow the feet to breathe and avoid any rubbing or sores. You must of course take them off immediately after you return from a walk, to air them, and to rinse them from time to time in warm water.

Since a dog does not sweat through its skin, it cools down its body by panting. The only sweat glands that it possesses are situated on the pads of its paws.

By dabbing the pads of your old dog's paws from time to time with cottonwool soaked in surgical spirit (by prescription from your vet), you will reinforce the old dog's soles naturally, helping him to tackle the hard ground more valiantly: but watch out for your carpet, as this product is highly coloured.

⊕ **Claws** With a young energetic dog these normally wear down during the course of a walk or running around, but with an elderly dog they have much less chance of wearing down. You must therefore trim them yourself to prevent the dog going lame or wounding itself by catching them in something. Pay attention though. The dog's claws are very strong, paring them must be done using a special pair of clippers with a 'guillotine' action, so that you don't crush or damage the claw. Most importantly, do not cut into the live part of the nail, which will make the dog bleed copiously. It is highly recommended that you always keep a supply of haemostatic powder at home to stop any accidental bleeding immediately.

As the vestiges of a fifth or even a sixth digit, the dew claw needs to be watched particularly carefully because, since it does not touch the ground, it cannot be worn down in a natural way and therefore has a tendency to grow into the flesh, producing serious lesions.

⊕ **The anal glands** These are often overlooked by owners, but through swelling they can cause discomfort to the animal, which then begins to drag its bottom along the ground. Pressing the area around the anus, using a paper towel is generally enough to soothe the dog, but beware of the very strong smell.

Nutrition

An elderly dog's diet is one of the most efficient ways of fighting against the onslaught of old age. Obviously you should not wait for the first signs of senility before becoming concerned about your companion's nutritional requirements. As soon as it passes into the category of 'senior', you should start giving it a specific type of food. This change of food should be introduced gradually over ten days or so, reducing its old type of food little by little and replacing it with the new: too brutal a transition will sometimes end up with the dog refusing to eat at all or having digestive problems such as diarrhoea.

⊕ **Energy requirements for an elderly dog** These are about 12 per cent less than for an adult dog. The slowing down of the metabolism, the lessening of physical activity and an intestine which is becoming 'lazy' demand new proportions of energy-giving supplies.

• **Proteins:** Contrary to received knowledge, these must absolutely not be suppressed in the diet, but simply selected with more care for their 'very high quality' (poultry, milk casein, fishmeal). Note: in the case of renal insufficiency, if the proteins can be reduced, most probably a hypophosphoric diet (low in phosphorous) will be prescribed by the vet.

• **Carbohydrates:** While an elderly dog may need the same amount of sugars as an adult dog, you must take steps to ban 'rapid' sugars (sugar, sweets, pastries) and instead use 'slow' sugars (starch). Note: in the case of diabetic animals, the vet will establish a specific diet to control the glycaemia, that is to say, the level of sugar in the blood.

• **Lipids:** These must be decreased in order to prevent obesity. But you must be careful not to suppress the 'useful fats' containing essential fatty acids (Omega 3 and Omega 6). Gammalinoleic acid (GLA) can no longer be absorbed in an optimal way by the ageing dog, so it is a good idea to introduce it into its diet in the form of oil of onager, borage or blackcurrant seeds (cassis). A combination of fish oil and borage oil produces a healthy and elastic skin as well as a supple, shiny coat. Linoleic acid, which is essential for the maintenance of the skin's waterproofing properties in old dogs, can be provided by adding a little sunflower oil to their diet.

- **Vitamins:** Vitamin A is essential for regulating keratinisation and for the secretion of sebum (note, too little vitamin A, just as too much, will result in a decrease in the skin's resistance to infections). Vitamins E and C are the 'top form' vitamins for an elderly dog; their antioxidant effect helps the animal to fight infectious diseases, cancers and cataract (a vitamin E deficit almost always shows up as erythema and a scaly skin). By stimulating the immune system and acidifying the urine, vitamin C is a considerable help in combating bladder infections (bacteria find it difficult to increase rapidly in an acidic milieu). Vitamins in group B, which are equally indispensable since they are hydrosoluble, should be provided in a greater quantity for an old dog, which urinates more frequently, thus eliminating them more quickly (a vitamin B deficit is almost always manifested in a dry, brittle coat and alopecia).

Very large breeds (Saint Bernard, German mastiff, Irish wolfhound, Anatolian sheepdog) which begin aging early should be supported with vitamins E and C much earlier on (near the age of five) than small and medium breeds.

- **Minerals:** These should be used with caution. While iron and zinc are effective in stimulating the organism's defences and help to combat anaemia, sodium (salt) is forbidden for animals with cardiac problems, and phosphorus must be reduced for those suffering from a renal insufficiency. Note that excessive consumption of foods rich in calcium, copper and phytates can prevent the dog's body from absorbing the amount of zinc necessary for the synthesis of its DNA (Desoxyribonucleic acid), its fatty acids and its pigmentation.

- **Fibres:** These play an essential role in the passage through the intestines. It appears that the combination of soluble fibres (like beet pulp) and insoluble fibres (like maize) are ideal for keeping the colon in good health and the production of stools of a normal consistency. Note, however, it is important never to give too much, for an excess of alimentary fibre can lead to partial or total non-assimilation of a food.

Of the possible different types of food, homemade meals based on fresh produce and leftovers are no longer appropriate for old dogs. It is in fact very difficult to give a good balance to an old dog's meals: numerous protein and vitamin deficiencies are often noticed while lipids and minerals appear in far too great a quantity. From a strictly economic point of view, providing the nutritional supplements that are indispensable for the dog's health make homemade meals 'too expensive'. Good quality factory-made foods, which have been specially researched by canine nutritionists, are perfectly adapted to the new exigencies of the elderly dog. Certain brands go even as far as developing a specific food range for animals suffering from various ailments, such as obesity, cardiac insufficiency, kidney or liver insufficiency, arthritis or digestive problems.

⊕ **Tinned and semi-moist foods** Although having the same nutritional qualities as dry food, these are not really recommended because they make it difficult to keep the teeth clean. The food clings to the gums and will cause bacteria to proliferate. It goes without saying that very old dogs which no longer have teeth or are suffering from gingivitis will prefer this type of food which is much easier to chew. In such cases you must clean out their mouth after each meal.

🐕 It is worthwhile reading the packaging of dog food carefully: 'with meat' indicates that meat of some sort is present: however 'meaty' means only that it has the flavour of meat and probably contains mostly soybean.

⊕ **Biscuits** As well as helping to keep the teeth free of tartar, dry food has a quite substantial effect in exercising the cheek muscles by making the dog chew. Biscuits labelled 'premium' which are more concentrated and made with produce of better quality, mean that the dog can be offered the nutritional elements that it needs and at the same time its usual ration can be decreased by half, thus lessening the burden on the stomach and avoiding digestive problems among the most gluttonous, such as stomach torsion which is always possible among big dogs.

Light, with added vitamins, proteins, enriched with fluorine or calcium, flavoured with meat juices or mint, descaling agents, stimulants or tranquilisers, artificial bones pose a new problem for dog owners: which to choose?

🐕 Biscuits should be kept if possible in their original packaging away from light, or better still in a container specially made for this, for plastic bags or packaging that is poorly sealed allow different odours to creep in (chemical products, petrol or paint fumes, washing powders etc.) which is always unpleasant for the dog.

⊕ **The special case of bones** Even when they are old, dogs remain very partial to bones; you must, however, completely exclude this small pleasure from their diet. Unfortunately, it can sometimes happen that fragments of bone get stuck in the wall of the intestines, preventing the animal from producing normal stools. The faeces which are retained accumulate and harden more and more until they obstruct the intestine completely. This very serious constipation, known as 'obstipation', during which one sees the poor animal trying desperately to do his duty, ends up with one having to have recourse to a vet for three or four days in order to get rid of the intestinal occlusion.

Bones and other toys made from hide should be adapted to the size of the animal's mouth and thrown away without hesitation when they have been chewed sufficiently, to prevent any risk of the dog swallowing them accidentally, which could choke or suffocate a very greedy dog.

⊕ **The number of meals a day** For old dogs this is similar to that for puppies. The intestine has a tendency to become lazy with age, and a single large meal once a day can lead to the animal having chronic constipation. Much preferred is to divide up the same quantity of food into three 'small' daily meals at fixed times in the morning, midday and evening which will not only have the advantage of stimulating the intestinal function but equally avoid the risks of bloating, fermentation and of a heavy stomach.

It is sometimes necessary to moisten the biscuits slightly with a little broth to increase the dog's appetite and to make them easier to chew. You must always leave out a bowl of clean fresh water for the dog (and renew it every day). If the dog has a chance to go out into a large garden or lives in a spacious house, you can cunningly leave several bowls of water for it at strategic points at places where it likes to go so that it can quench its thirst whenever it needs. Let us not forget that, for all living things, water is the most important and indispensable nutrient for survival.

A chance to live longer

I have sometimes asked myself why, in fact, dogs have such a brief life, and I am satisfied to conclude that it is through compassion for the human race, for if we suffer so much when we lose a dog after ten or twelve years of companionship, what would it be like were it to live for double that time?

SIR WALTER SCOTT

While, for the moment, there is no question of a miraculous canine 'fountain of youth' where all one has to do is to plunge the dog into the water for it to rediscover its vigour of a two-year-old, nevertheless there are some relatively little explored fields that can give your faithful companion a longer life in a significant way.

⊕ **Sterilisation** Although this has a bad reputation, this surgical operation, when it has been properly considered and reflected upon, brings a certain comfort to an animal which is not destined for breeding. Ideally this should be carried out before the dog's puberty, at around 6-8 months for small breeds and 10-12 months for the larger ones. Contrary to received ideas, sterilisation in no way affects the growth and development of the dog which will remain just a bit more youthful than an 'entire' one. The anthropomorphic notion that a dog or a bitch absolutely must have experience of coupling in order to be a well balanced animal has absolutely no scientific foundation.

• **For females** spaying (removal of the ovaries, the Fallopian tubes and womb) will avoid all the problems connected with being on heat (bleeding, excitation, attraction of male dogs...) as well as the risks of unwanted litters, phantom pregnancies, vaginal infections, metritis (inflammation of the uterus), pyometra (womb infections), mammary tumours, cancer of the genital area, diabetes...

• **For males** castration (removal of the testicles from the scrotum onwards) is also believed to be beneficial not only in preventing pathologies of the testicles and prostate but also in calming behavioural problems (marking with urine, excitation, running off, fighting with other dogs), most often due to the production of testosterone (the male sexual hormone) among dogs which have not had the operation.

• **The risks** of putting on weight, an argument advanced by the anti-sterilisation movement, can easily be regulated by an appropriate diet and a little exercise.

Records of canine longevity have always been established by sterilised dogs. More than 70 per cent of those which have not had the operation end their life without ever having had a litter.

⊕ **Alternative medicine** This has been very fashionable as far as human health is concerned, for a number of years, and now it is beginning to make an appearance in veterinary medicine. Much less aggressive than traditional treatments, these methods are, incontestably, being called into play a more and more important role in the treatment of elderly dogs.

• **Homeopathy** This is certainly the best known of alternative medicines and is based on the method of 'like with like', that is to say the remedy is similar to the illness, but administered in very weak doses, so that it releases a defensive reaction in the organism. Using substances of animal, vegetable and mineral origin, veterinary homeopathy is naturally inspired by human homeopathy. For maximum efficacy, the treatment must be perfectly adapted to each individual, so vets have applied Professor Vannier's typology and produced a classification of three main morphological types.

The Carbonics such as the Bouvier des Flandres, the Swiss bouviers, the mastiff, the Pyrenean mountain dog, Saint Bernard, Tibetan mastiff, Newfoundland and Leonberger, and all the big mountain-type dogs or similar are robust, rustic, solidly planted on their limbs, conscious of their

Chief among the 'carbonic' breeds, the Tibetan mastiff is nick-named 'Dog Nine' by the Tibetans who have noticed that the bitches very often first come on heat at the age of nine months, have litters of nine pups and a lifespan of nine years.

strength and their power; generally resistant to illness in youth, once they become 'senior' they become prone to problems of obesity, arthritis, urea, diabetes, liver, eczema.

The Fluorics such as the Chihuahua, Pug, Cavalier King Charles, Bull terrier, Lhasa Apso, Continental miniature spaniel, Bichon frise, Pekingese and all the small breed dogs are physically less solid; their teeth are often poorly implanted, rapidly attract tartar, their joints are more fragile. Once they are 'senior', they develop problems with the heart and ligaments as well as numerous behavioural problems.

The Phosphorics like the Whippet, Greyhound, Deerhound, Afghan, Galgo, Collie, Dobermann and all the other dogs of similar breed are slender, svelte, nervous and hypersensitive. Very active in their youth, they need a rich diet of very high quality. The 'seniors' develop frail intestines; have attacks of diarrhoea and dehydrate. Sensitive to the cold and draughts, they are equally prone to bronchitis.

Quite obviously, a dog can belong to several morphological types at the same time, for example, the French bulldog, which although it has a fluoric stature has the hypersensitivity of a phosphoric, and not forgetting mongrels, which by definition are the result of mixed breeding. In these circumstances, if the morphological type is relatively easy to recognise, the owner's role is important in outlining his companion's character type to the homeopathic vet in order to help him to prescribe, from among the 1300 homeopathic products currently available the one or the several that are necessary to combat the problems to which its type or types predispose it.

The soul of a 'phosphoric' in the body of 'fluoric' is how the French bulldog is described. Its extreme sensitivity is its dominant characteristic.

Whether it is a 'papillon,' with pricked ears or one with floppy ears, the Continental miniature spaniel, like all Fluorics, can, in spite of its dental problems, savour life until a very advanced age. Below, a genuine pure-blood of the canine world, the Dobermann is the archetypal Phosphoric dog, its lifespan averages about 12 years.

- **Isotherapy** is a therapeutic method very similar to homeopathy. There are generally two types, which can be distinguished through the source of the extract used.

Auto-isotherapy consists of giving the sick dog dilutions extracted from its own physiological or pathological secretions (this technique is slightly similar to that of vaccines). While this therapy seems fairly popular in the United States, it is little practised in Britain, and in France the manufacture of auto-isotherapeutic extracts has actually been banned since 22 June 1998.

Hetero-isotherapy consists of giving the dog dilutions not coming from its own body but from its immediate environment, and which have a quite obvious connection with the recognised symptoms of its allergy.

- **Oligotherapy** relies on oligo-elements, that is to say on metals of which there are trace elements in the body. These metals play a large part in helping the release of certain reactions in the organism. Just as in homeopathy, the oligo-elements are prescribed by the vet according to the pathological symptoms but also according to the dog's 'personality'. Let us mention for example:

SILVER given as an anti-infection agent
COPPER to stimulate expressions of self-defence
FLUORINE as a catalyst for metabolising calcium
LITHIUM for its action on behaviour problems
MAGNESIUM to counter pain and decalcification
PHOSPHORUS to calm spasms…

- **Phytotherapy** is certainly the oldest medicine known to man, the power of plants as a cure having been discovered at the dawn of mankind. Around 400 BC, Hippocrates was already using some 250 medicinal plants in his repertory, classifying them according to their healing, diuretic, purgative or vomitory properties. Modern phytotherapy puts numerous vegetal extracts at the vet's disposal in the form of capsules, tablets, powders and herbal teas that are easy to administer. Note, truly competent phytotherapists being very rare, it would be prudent to limit oneself to plants that are widespread before testing their efficacy. A few from memory are:

FOXGLOVE (*Digitalis purpurea*) to ease the elimination of urine

MADDER (*Rubia tinctoria*) to treat cystitis

HAWKWEED (*Pilosella*) as a diuretic to lower the level of urea

SEQUOIA (*Sequoia gigantea*) to firm and rejuvenate tissues

SILVER BIRCH SAP used as an anti-allergy, pain killer, anti-arthritis

MARIGOLD (*Calendula*) for its anti-infection properties

LIME (*Tilia*) used as a sedative and anti-spasmodic

• **Algotherapy** This is similar to phytotherapy except that it uses exclusively seaweed in the form of tablets, capsules or powdered food. Based on certain properties that certain seaweeds possess to absorb and concentrate numerous mineral elements contained in sea water in their thallus (a sort of root by which the seaweed attaches itself). For old dogs it can be a very good food supplement since it can gently get round some deficiencies in iron, zinc, copper, magnesium, potassium, fluoride or sulphur.

• **Aromatherapy** Despite the lack of enthusiasm it arouses, this is one of the most efficacious medicines there are. Based on the properties of essential oils (EO) extracted after distillation from aromatic plants and trees, it consists of ingesting (using drops, oral sprays, pastes to swallow), inhaling (diffusers, inhalers) or simply putting on the animal's skin (balms, creams, pomades) aromatic molecules which will release its organism's defences by stimulating them. So:

EO of BASIL (*Ocimum basilicum*) is a powerful anti-spasmodic which aids digestion

EO of CYPRESS (*Cupressus sempervirens*) is very versatile. It is simultaneously an antitussive, antispasmodic, a neurotonic and a general balance restorer.

EO of SCENTED GERANIUM (*Pelargonium graveolens*) is very invigorating, and also useful for skin troubles

EO of CLOVE (*Eugenia carophyllata*) is an analgesic, an antiseptic

and excellent stimulant for the brain

EO of MARJORAM (*Origanum majorana*) is a good anti-depressant, gastric stimulant and regulates the appetite

EO of PEPPERMINT (*Mentha piperita*) is an anti-vomitory, but also a tonic when it is used as a diffuser

EO of THYME (*Thymus vulgaris*) is a psychological tonic and a general tonic

Shampoos, bath gels and other beauty products with evocative names, commercialised by certain cosmetic laboratories under the label of 'aromatherapy' must in no way be confused with real essential oils. Although hypoallergenic and containing some natural extracts of plants, these products are in fact no more than humble cleansing agents uniquely for washing, perfuming and giving a glow to the skin.

• **Clay therapy** Although it has almost fallen into oblivion, this method which uses the disinfecting, healing and anti-rheumatic properties of silica (*Silicea*) contained in clay, was much used by the ancient Egyptians, Greeks and Romans. It is moreover interesting to note that many wild animals (wolves, bears, wild boar...) when they are wounded immediately roll in certain kinds of mud to cauterise their wound.

Itim, an eleven-year-old Coton de Tuléar, fighting fit thanks to clay therapy

The legend goes that the famous 'Peloïd' (therapeutic mud) which made the town of Dax's fortune was accidentally discovered by a Roman centurion's dog.

Clay, preferably green clay, is recommended in the form of a poultice for old dogs suffering from incapacitating rheumatism, bronchitis and chronic suppurations. A small amount of 'Zeolite' clay diluted in drinking water will rapidly calm chronic diarrhoea.

• **Fumigants** are a very old therapeutic technique which is very similar to aromatherapy. Developed by Indian and African tribes after the discovery of fire, the animal is subjected to vapours or fumes coming from medicinal plants. There are two types of fumigation:

Moist fumigation where the plants are boiled in water to obtain an aromatic vapour

Dry fumigation where the plants are burnt directly on hot coals to obtain an aromatic smoke.

• **Therapeutic incenses** used by the Chinese and Tibetans from time immemorial represent the spiritual version of fumigation. If their therapeutic power seems pretty limited, they can nevertheless contribute to creating a calm and peaceful atmosphere which, by de-stressing the master, in turn de-stresses the old dog, always attuned to atmospheres and states of mind: As we say in France: 'A *maître zen, chien serein*' – 'With a Zen master, a serene dog'.

⊕ **Acupuncture** Although this type of therapy is a direct descendant of traditional Chinese medicine that is more than 4,000 years old, it did not truly start to be developed in the veterinary world until the end of the 1970s. Based on the stimulation of very precise points in the animal's body, using needles (or heat, or cold laser, or even simple fingertip massage (known as digi-puncture), it leads the vital force (*chi*) to the heart of each organ through virtual channels which are conductors of energy (meridians) which connect the points between them. Acupuncture can treat joint, muscle and tendon problems in spectacular fashion, as well as behavioural problems (anxiety, depression), circulation problems (hypertension, oedema), digestion (constipation, diarrhoea, vomiting), and respiratory problems (breathlessness, bronchitis), the urinary tract (cystitis) and skin disorders (dermatosis, eczema) etc.

There is a technique in acupuncture which consists of stimulating certain very particular points in a permanent way through the implant of minute 'gold pearls', which make the brain produce endorphins which curb the pain.
Note that the acupuncture points in a dog are not at all the same as in man, who has more than 800 of them.

⊕ **Stimulating the brain** This is something very simple to do in many areas. It is real behavioural therapy which will reawaken the old dog's interest in its environment and its social group, and prevent it from sinking into depression and boredom. The animal's 'morale' has a direct bearing on his 'will to live' and is at least as important for a long lifespan as his physical well being: *mens sana in corpore sano*.

• **Learning new skills** A dog's acquirement of skills is much less permanent than a human's, and so the old dog has a tendency to forget gradually what it has learned in its youth. So it seems it is very necessary to give the dog some short reminders of its basic education (Come, Sit, Lie down, Stand up). During these very short sessions (no more than five minutes), the dog will rediscover the pleasure of the 'connection' with its master.

Practised every day as a game, a basic education will enable Massai, an American Staffordshire Bull terrier to stay in tune with the outside world, while preserving a privileged dialogue with his master.

You can also re-energise your old companion's olfactory and visual memories by playing different types of games of the hunt-the-thimble sort with it:

Game 1 Place three flowerpots upside down in front of the dog, placing his ball very ostentatiously under one of them (you can use a biscuit or a small piece of cheese instead which will be much more stimulating), then encourage the dog to search for and discover the 'treasure' with a pat of his paw or with his nose. You can make the exercise more complicated by burying the object that must be found close by, without the dog knowing.

Game 2 Having hidden a small slice of sausage in one of your hands, hold each fist in turn in front of the dog's nose, one after the other, then hold them out at the same time 50 cm apart. As soon as the dog is interested in the hand which has the sausage, let it have it and warmly praise it at the same time.

Game 3 First make a few holes in a plastic cube or in an old tennis ball (depending on the dog's size), and then put some biscuits inside it. This 'food safe' is then given to the animal which must use its imagination and synchronise its movements in order to retrieve the biscuits from inside the cube: it can try shaking it, rolling it, or making the holes bigger.

Game 4 Put a stopper in one end of a plastic (or PVC) tube about ten centimetres in diameter and then place the dog's ball inside, or some titbit that it is very keen on before standing the pipe three or four metres in front of it. Once the animal has succeeded in picking out the object of its desire by knocking the tube over, you begin the game again, this time lying the tube on its side (with the titbit or ball tucked well at the back), which will force the dog to change its strategy in order to reach its goal: it will have to pick up the tube in its mouth, roll it, squeeze it with its paws, push its nose into it. In the case of a small dog, a plastic bottle which has had the neck carefully cut off will do the job perfectly.

Game 5 First show the dog a big crust of dry bread, then cover it with a bit of old carpet or a carpet square (big and heavy enough for the crust to be completely covered), then encourage the dog to look for the bread. The animal will then have to coordinate its movements, whether it is scratching the 'bump' until it has brought the crust to the edge of the carpet, or lifting the carpet without standing on it.

You can also give the animal a sense of responsibility by giving it an errand, like making it carry a little basket to the house, or a rolled newspaper or its own ball on its regular outings.

A handful of biscuits slipped inside a simple square plastic container (for holding liquids) reveals Heming's cunning. Heming is a thirteen-year-old Irish setter

Violent games and highly competitive sports which your dog has long enjoyed must be forbidden once it enters the third age

These games which at first sight may seem puerile are actually very effective in re-awakening what the psychologists call 'crystallised intelligence', that is to say, they oblige the animal to remember strategies that it has already learned. Once these neurones are reconnected, it will soon be waiting for these little games and will be clamouring for them. Knowing your dog's 'personality' and preferences, you can then adapt and invent new games *ad infinitum*. After only a few sessions, you will often notice a kind of jubilation in your dog, which is happy to have relearned the learning process. Its capacity to learn will be stimulated, its sociability will automatically be reinforced. The ethologist Konrad Lorenz (who won the Nobel Prize for Physiology in 1973) said that, among all animals, games and the learning of games not only led to the manipulation of inanimate objects but also to social skills.

Whatever results you achieve, it is very important to increase your dog's standing after each exercise by stroking it and praising it so that it still feels useful and necessary to its master. (Anyone who has ever looked his or her old worn-out dog in the eye when it comes home feeling useless after treatment of one kind or another will have some idea of the distress of an animal that knows it is incapable and useless.)

• **The arrival of a new companion** This is an excellent stimulus for an elderly dog, which will have to make new physical and psychological efforts to maintain its status in the new pack. Note, it is sometimes necessary to take certain precautions, for even if it is relatively easy to make an older dog accept a new puppy, it is not always so with animals of the same sex. The choice of a newcomer will depend directly on the aging dog's character, the aim being to stimulate the old dog and not annoy or terrorise it. You must therefore avoid a situation where two dominant dogs are living together, or two dogs of disproportionate sizes, so that you can limit the risk of an accident or conflicts of hierarchy that are always possible. Why not profit from the occasion by adopting a calm and tranquil old dog from a rescue centre (generally these dogs are sterilised and in good health) and they would also be happy to finish their days in a proper pack?

 It is always wise to present the new arrival to your old dog on neutral territory (a wood, a park, the garden of a friend) in order to avoid a possible confrontation with your old dog defending its territory. When you return to the house, the two companions will already have sniffed each other and played together and will no longer be strangers at all....

A lively and particularly robust country dog, this Border terrier puppy will be a boost and a salvation for this elderly, eleven-year-old Irish wolfhound.

Apart from breeds for which it is normal to recommend grooming, or when it is a question of an animal that has been wounded or has eczema, it is futile, even dangerous, to clip an old animal. Because of its coat and its undercoat, its fur has in fact a capacity for regulating warmth that, by trapping air, insulates the dog from the cold as well as from the heat.

• **Avoid long separations** Thirty per cent of old dogs die while their master is on holiday. If you cannot take your animal with you, the best solution is to leave it in its familiar environment and ask someone whom you can trust, whom it knows and values, to come and feed it and walk it several times a day. You could also ask a homesitter (see under Useful Addresses). There are more and more of these organisations who generally use 'hand-picked' retired people (inquiries have been made into their moral standing, criminal record, retirement status) selected for their abilities and of course their love of animals.

If there is no other way but to use kennels, you should be extremely vigilant when you select one, go there beforehand with your dog in order to avoid nasty surprises and gradually accustom the future lodger (you must ensure that there is a vet whom the premises can call upon). Do not forget to ask for a receipt on headed paper which gives details, in addition to the payments you have already made of the price per day, the date on which the animal was taken in, its identichip or tattoo number as well as its eventual special daily diet or, if necessary, its dosages of medicine. Without these precautions, should the dog disappear, any help would be very difficult. To avoid this sort of litigation, ideally you should get a vet to issue a certificate of good health for the dog before you confine it to kennels.

The person to whom one confides the care of the dog is totally responsible for it. The owner of the animal, or the person who is using it while it is in his care is responsible for any damage the animal causes, whether the animal is in his care or whether it has become lost or has strayed.

• **Keep showing your dog your affection** and your compassion, something often overlooked by owners, but which however is of prime importance in the animal's psychological well-being, now that it is frail, old and possibly ill. Think about it: if dogs that are used for therapy in some hospitals, hospices and old people's homes can succeed in bolstering morale in sick humans by bringing them out of their isolation, the same must also be true the other way round. Stroking and talking to your animal comfortingly and frequently, on a daily basis, is bound to help calm its heartbeat and alleviate its stress and anxieties.

First aid for dogs

As responsible owner living with a mature dog, it is essential that you acquire some knowledge of first aid for dogs so that in situations of extreme urgency which require rapid treatment to keep the animal alive, you can cope before the vet arrives.

⊕ **How to stop a haemorrhage:** If the dog is involved in an accident, it could have a severed artery, in which case blood will be pouring out in abundance. You must, immediately, press very hard on the wound, if possible with sterile compresses, clean dusters or failing these, simply use your hand or fist. If the flow of blood does not slow down, or stop by forming a clot, you must intervene at the nearest pressure point to the wound (i.e., one situated between the wound and the heart) and press very strongly with three fingers of one hand or with both thumbs until the bleeding stops. The principle pressure points are situated in the groin, the axillae (the equivalent of a human's armpits), the base of the tail just above the anus, on the neck – in the groove beside the windpipe, and where the lower jaw joins the ear (the condyle of the maxillary joints).

You will need to relax the pressure every five to six minutes to allow blood to irrigate the tissues around the wound.

The lead is a bond of love that can be multiplied
A cuddle is the best form of therapy

When it is a limb that is haemorrhaging, use a compress dressing (several compresses bound with a bandage) or a tourniquet (a piece of string, a belt, a scarf or a wristwatch on a strap) these will be easy to put in place 'upstream' from the wound.

🐕 **You must not leave a tourniquet in place for more than two hours.**

⊕ **How to use cardiac massage:** In the case of a cardiac arrest, this method will help to restart the heart beat. You must lie the dog on its right side (so that you can get at the heart which is towards the left side of the thoracic cavity), then place the palm of one hand flat on its flank and press on this hand intermittently with your other hand, so that you stimulate the heart. It is easier to keep a rhythm if you count, this will help to keep the pressure regular: one, two, press; one, two, press; one, two, press…

A reanimating technique that is simple and easy to apply, and that every owner should know

⊕ **Artificial respiration:** As soon as you realise that the dog is no longer breathing, open its mouth and pull the tongue forward to make sure that there is no object (such as a bone, toy, ball or plastic bag) obstructing the lungs. If there is nothing, use artificial respiration. To do this, keep the dog's mouth closed with one hand, while you breathe slowly into its nostrils using the other hand as a 'funnel'. Use the same rhythm as the dog's own normal breathing. You must continue with the artificial respiration until the dog starts to breathe on its own again or until the vet arrives.

⊕ **Heimlich's manoeuvre:** This is commonly used for humans when food goes down the wrong way, and adapted for a dog the technique helps the animal to spit out an object obstructing its lungs. With your legs spread, place yourself behind your dog, then, after squeezing its abdomen under the ribs with both your arms, lift up the dog's hindquarters, simultaneously squeezing its belly hard (pushing the diaphragm against the lungs will create a strong pressure that will expel the object). If your dog has a small build you can easily lift it up, but for big dogs it is better to leave their front paws on the ground (like a wheelbarrow).

⊕ **How to make a dog vomit:** This has been found to be very useful when the animal has swallowed a noncorrosive object (pills or tablets intended for its owner, for example). If the traditional finger down the throat has not produced the desired result, you must make the dog swallow either some very salty water or a solution using soap flakes to start the dog vomiting.

Contrary to received ideas, you must never give a dog milk if it has swallowed poison, nor make it vomit after it has swallowed a corrosive product (such as acid, soda, disinfectant, cleaning fluid or paint). All this will achieve is to make the lesions bigger, because the product will then be passed over the same affected tissues a second time. In every case, it is imperative to take the packaging of the product the dog has swallowed to the vet, along with the dog.

⊕ **How to lower a dog's temperature:** When your dog is feverish, if you can lower its temperature, you can prevent it from dehydrating. In the case of large dogs, a garden hose will do the trick perfectly. Gently spray the whole of the dog's body for three or four minutes, reassuring the dog at the same time. If your dog is small, wrapping it in a wet floor cloth or a wet towel will produce the same effect. You can also rub the belly and axillae (armpits) with 90 degree or 70 degree proof alcohol, which will instantly cool the dog down as it evaporates.

⊕ **How to put on a makeshift splint:** Putting on a splint will help to immobilise a fractured limb while you are taking the dog to the vet's. Depending on the dog's size, you can immobilise its paw with a small board (from a crate, for example), a piece of cardboard, or even better, a rolled newspaper or magazine which is folded into a gutter shape, and held in place with a bandage, or sticky tape, Scotch tape or a piece of string.

System D to immobilise a fractured paw, which will prevent the dog from suffering while it is being transported

⊕ **How to cope with an epileptic fit:** Although the convulsions (extreme contractions, rapid pedalling movements) only last a few minutes and will generally come to an end by themselves, during an attack you must put a wedge of cushions, blankets or coats around the dog to stop it wounding itself. Pull the dog's tongue out of its mouth to prevent any risk of suffocating and if possible leave it in a calm place in a dark room, as stimulations of sound and light only make the fit worse. Shouting at the dog or ordering it to stop or to calm down is completely futile, for the dog is totally cut off from the outside world.

🐕 **Convulsions can also occur after a dog has swallowed poisonous products containing methaldehyde or strychnine (e.g. slug pellets or rat poison). This is very serious and the dog must be examined urgently by a vet.**

Enclosed in a car, even in the shade, a large dog will rapidly use the oxygen available inside the cabin

⊕ **Heat stroke:** Heatstroke can happen to any dog and can often be fatal in elderly dogs. Unlike man, a dog does not possess many sweat glands, and so it regulates its body temperature through breathing. When it can no longer breathe fresh air normally (enclosed in a car or tied up in full sunshine, for example), it begins to pant more and more rapidly, its body temperature quickly rises to more than 41 degrees C, its head becomes boiling, its tongue goes purple, and it could well suffer a stroke. If its owner reacts quickly, he can still save his companion by plunging the dog into cold water or spraying it abundantly with a hose pipe and rolling it in a wet cloth full of ice cubes, or by rubbing it with 90 degree proof alcohol – brandy will do – and taking it to a shady spot exposed to draughts or a breeze.

It is easy to avoid heatstroke as long as you follow the following rules:
• **Never leave the dog alone in a car, even in shade and even with the windows half open**
• **Never make it play or run in full sun**
• **Find it a shady corner to lie down**
• **Always leave it a bowl of fresh water**
• **Cool the dog down from time to time by spraying it with a hosepipe, plant spray or an vaporiser**
• **Wet its paw pads by soaking its paws in a bowl of cool water**

⊕ **Gastric bloat or stomach torsion:** Big dogs are especially prone to this after too large a meal gulped down too quickly or after playing or making too intense an effort, and it is one of the most serious accidents that can happen. The symptoms, which are very alarming, are easy to spot: if the dog's stomach has just become twisted, it will stop all activity, suddenly appear very anxious, walk round and round in circles, begin to slaver abundantly and try to vomit, emitting groans but without achieving anything. When it finally stands still, its swollen stomach has become enormous, its skin stretched as tight as a drum. At this stage the animal is in danger of dying. You must alert the vet as soon as you can, so that he can prepare for surgical intervention as soon as the dog arrives. Depending on how serious the situation has become and the state of distension, a professional will have the choice between:

- **Oro-gastric catheterisation** that is to say, emptying the stomach with a supple rubber catheter which is passed down the animal's gullet
- **Using a trocar** – a sort of broad hyperdermic needle which is stuck directly into the abdomen and right into the stomach, and through which the accumulated gases then escape.
- **Gastroplexy** – a very difficult operation which involves opening the dog from the sternum to the pubis in order to reposition the stomach and the surrounding organs.

If , alas, you find yourself in an isolated spot when the accident happens, or if the dog is in such an advanced state of shock that you cannot transport it, the owner must simply go for it, and puncture the dog's stomach to release the gas from the fermentation. For that you need to cut 3 or 4 cms through the skin behind the ribs (about three fingertips from the last rib) using a sharp tool (cutter, razor blade, very sharp knife). The stomach, which at this stage will almost completely fill the abdomen, will not be difficult to find. The incision must be unequivocal and precise, the animal itself being momentarily insensible, because of its state of shock. Once the decompression is finished (there is a characteristic smell and the stomach will deflate), you must douse the wound with Betadine, cover it if possible with a clean cloth and take the dog as soon as possible to a vet who will complete the procedure.

You can considerably reduce the risk of your dog getting bloat or suffering from a twisted stomach by:
- Leaving it for an hour of peace and quiet before its meals and for two hours afterwards
- Dividing its daily ration into several meals in order not to overload its stomach
- Giving the dog 'premium' type food, which although having the same nutritional value takes up three times less volume than a homemade meal;
- Raising the dog's dish and water bowl so that it absorbs the least possible air when it is drinking or eating;

- Preventing it from imbibing a huge quantity of water in one go when it comes in from playing or running
- Isolating it from other dogs (the pack) to prevent it from competing in gluttony.

Basic first aid kit

To be able to care for all those small everyday cuts and sores and be able to rise to the event when a more serious accident occurs, it is a good idea to have a first aid kit at hand in the house or in the boot of your car when you are on holiday. It should have:

⊕ Instruments and materials

- **A muzzle** to prevent the wounded dog biting someone
- **Nail clippers**
- **Tweezers** to remove ticks, thorns and grass seeds
- **A safety razor to shave hair around a wound**
- **A pair of scissors**
- **A trocar** to be able to purge the stomach directly in the event of gastric torsion
- **Three plastic syringes** of different capacities to administer liquid doses of medicine
- **A medical thermometer**
- **Sterile compresses**
- **Adhesive tape**
- **A cotton bandage**
- **Elastoplast**

⊕ Basic products

- **Washing soap** to clean and disinfect wounds, especially in the case of a bite
- **Betadine** (or iodine alcohol) as an antiseptic
- **Hydrogen peroxide** as a disinfectant and to encourage vomiting (one soup spoonful to every 10 kg of live weight)

- **An antibiotic spray** (or cream) for local infections
- **A hydrocortisone cream** to treat small inflammations
- **Physiological salt solution** to clean eyes and nostrils
- **A tube of Vaseline** to lubricate the anus will make it easier to insert a medical thermometer; also useful for covering ticks, causing them to fall off
- **White spirit** for removing ticks

⊕ **Specific products** If you are aware of your old dog's past medical history and its known weaknesses, it should be a simple matter to foresee what adapted medications may be needed to counter these.

Before your dog ever becomes ill, you can, cunningly, get it used to taking medications by giving it a 'placebo' from time to time, such as a little biscuit or some sugared water. Then, when your dog is genuinely sick, this precaution will mean that your animal, which is already ill, will avoid becoming even more disturbed by its master's strange behaviour towards it.

⊕ **How to give tablets** This can be done either by concealing the tablet inside a meatball or some melted cheese, which all dogs go mad for, or being a bit firmer and making the dog open its mouth by pressing on the edge of the lips (just behind the fangs, then placing the

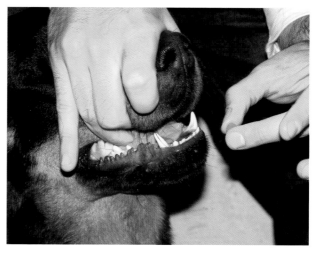

Watch out for the crafty ones who hide the tablet in their cheeks so that they can spit it out later

tablet as far back as you can in its throat before keeping its mouth shut and massaging its neck until it swallows.

⊕ **How to dose with liquid:** This can be done by using a syringe (without the needle). Slip the end into the side of the mouth behind the molars. The liquid should be squirted in slowly so that the dog can swallow it without risk of choking.

⊕ **How to take a dog's temperature:** Taking the dog's temperature can be very useful in helping the vet to give a diagnosis. In the case of a persistent fever, taking the dog's temperature every six hours will establish how the fever is progressing. The fever will be classified as follows:

• **Continuous** when the temperature remains constant
• **Fluctuating** when there are periods when the temperature is very high, interspersed with periods when the temperature is normal
• **Remittent** when the temperature rises daily for a few hours.

The only reliable method of taking a dog's temperature is to use a medical thermometer which has been wiped with Vaseline and to insert half of it into the dog's rectum. (For small dogs you should use a paediatric medical thermometer). Keep the dog calm by stroking and reassuring it for one to two minutes to ensure that it does not break the thermometer by moving about, then you can read the tempera-ture immediately afterwards, which should not exceed 38.5 degrees C.

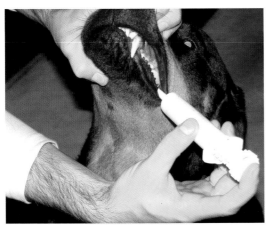

A few drops of beef stock or meat juice on the end of the syringe will help a dog accept the potion.

Separation

For this or any other dog
I believe in heaven, yes, I believe in heaven
Which I shall not enter, but where he will be waiting for me
Wagging his tail like a fan
To greet me with affection when I come.

PABLO NERUDA, *The separate rose*

Your dog's future

After years of complicity, fidelity and self-denial, sadly, the painful moment of separation must come. While this may happen in a totally natural way, with your old dog fading away without suffering in the evening of a happy, well fulfilled life, with you at its side, it may also be the outcome of a grave and difficult decision that you have had to make.

⊕ **Euthanasia** When the vet tells you that there is no new treatment to curb the fatal development of an illness and that his care can no longer lessen the pain, he will suggest putting the dog to sleep. This final injection, which will bring the dog's suffering to a close and at the same time allow it to finish its life with dignity can be considered as the final act of love and recognition that a responsible dog owner cannot refuse to what has been his most faithful companion for ten or fifteen years.

🐕 **Euthanasia must never be taken lightly or considered as a practical way of getting rid of an old dog that has become a burden. The law in no way exonerates the owner of his duty of care for his animal.**

Once the decision has been taken, you must not change your daily routine and must make sure that you do not show the animal how distressed and upset you are. In order to avoid making the dog anxious by taking it to the vet's surgery, it is better if the vet can come to the house. You must rally all your courage to be with your old companion right to the last second (that is the least you can do). To avoid the dog feeling any suffering the vet will administer a powerful sedative before injecting the fatal dose of anaesthetic. Breathing and the heart beat will stop very rapidly without the already unconscious animal being aware of anything.

Considered to be the first real animal cemetery for the general public in France, the dog cemetery at Asnières, created by Marguerite Durand and Georges Harnois in 1899, was classified as a historical monument in 1987. In Britain one of the oldest (which closed in 1915) is in Hyde Park which opened in 1880 and has 300 dogs' graves

Immediately after your dog has died, the question of what will happen to its remains arises. While the simplest solution is to leave the body of the animal with the vet who will arrange to have it cremated (in which case it will not be possible to retrieve the ashes), some owners nevertheless think it right to take care of their companion one last time.

⊕ **Individual cremation** will enable you to retrieve your dog's ashes, either in a simple bag so that you can scatter them somewhere, or in a decorated urn if you would like to keep them at home. For information, your vet can advise you or you can go to the local council office or go directly to a pet crematorium, of which there are around forty in the UK (see under Useful Addresses). The cost of an individual pet cremation is in the range of £60 to £120 and they can take up to four hours to complete.

⊕ **Burial in your garden** It is quite possible, but check with the draconian measures set out by the Environment Agency. The body should be buried at least one metre deep, at least ten metres from ponds and streams and one and a half metres from any underground water pipes. Once you have buried your dog, you are not allowed to exhume it. Do not bury it wrapped in plastic; far better to wrap it in its old blanket. The dog's owner must own the land.

⊕ **Animal cemeteries** There are many of these all over the country (see Useful addresses). Having bought or leased a plot (the cost is between £180 and £350 payable in a lump sum or in instalments), it will then be possible to visit your dog's grave.

⊕ **The virtual cemetery** There are several sites on the Internet which will accommodate a photograph of your companion together with a few words or a poem about it.

⊕ **Taxidermy** or the 'art of stuffing' which allows you to keep a 'living' memory of your companion animal is flourishing in the United States and Canada, but little taken up here nowadays, though in Victorian times it was quite popular. However, if you are interested, it will help if you can provide the taxidermist with several photos of your companion taken in a familiar setting, so that he can reconstitute the most faithful likeness of the dog's most favourite pose or posture. Note, however, prices can be quite high and it would be wise to have a written estimate before work begins (See Useful Addresses).

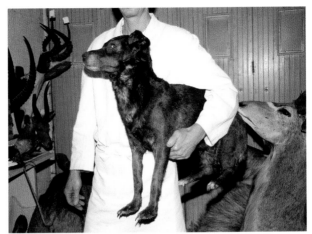

Stuffed about ten years ago by Vaillier (a taxidermy company in the Paris region) this 'seated' Labrador cross seems to be eternally waiting for the return of his master

According to the Environment Agency, dumping the body of an animal on the public highway, in ditches, or on rubbish tips or in open countryside is strictly forbidden.

On the death of a pedigree animal registered with the Kennel Club, the owner must notify them of the animal's demise.

Grieving for your dog

Grieving for your animal is not an easy matter. The immense pain that can be quite legitimately felt is sometimes ill understood by those around you. 'Can't you see,' the famous French novelist Emile Zola said, 'an animal's death is something very special. But, obviously, it cannot touch or affect anyone other than the one who loved it.'

After quite a long period, when time will have turned sadness into a gentle melancholy, the moment will come to fill the void by adopting a new little ball of fluff which, as we all know, 'will not be quite the same, nor completely different' but will, in turn, do the maximum to be loved.

Among the numerous poets and writers who have been able to translate the pain they felt at the loss of their four-footed friend, the French poet Francis Jammes is, for me, incontestably the one who has done so with the most modesty, dignity and emotion. May reading these few lines help a little in assuaging the grief of a tormented master or mistress.

You are dead, my faithful dog, my humble friend,
Fleeing from death as from a wasp,
You hid beneath the table. And in that brief,
Dismal moment you turned your eyes to me.

Ah, man's humdrum friend: may you be blessed!
You who were nourished by hunger your master shared
You who, on their pilgrimage, trotted beside
Archangel Raphael and the young Tobias.

Ah, my humble servant, my great example,
You who loved me as a saint loves his God!
The mystery of your dark complicity
Lives on in Paradise in innocence and joy.

Ah, My God, if You can give me the grace
To see You in Eternity, face to face,
Allow a poor dog, likewise, to gaze
Upon the one who was his earthly god.

FRANCIS JAMMES
'The church covered in leaves'
Clearings in the sky, 1905

Insurance

Of the animals who live with us, many are worthy of recognition, and more than all the others and most faithful to man is the dog.

PLINY THE ELDER, *Natural History*

The cost of surgical operations, which sometimes can be very high, and added to which the daily cost of hospitalisation and various vet's fees, have persuaded many owners of an elderly dog to take out insurance to cope with their companion's medical expenses.

Note: Do not confuse healthcare insurance with public liability insurance which is generally included in a comprehensive home insurance policy, and which covers only physical and material damage that the dog may inflict on others (you should also ensure that any contract contains this clause, and in addition advise the insurer if there is one or several dogs).

⊕ To be in insurable health

- The dog should not exceed the age limit imposed by the company at the time of signature of the contract
- Should be tattoed or microchipped (not often required)
- Vaccinated against Canine distemper, Hepatitis, Parvo virus enteritis
- Presented in a good state of general health

Many companies refuse to insure 'dangerous' dogs (as defined in the Dangerous Dogs Act 1991 [amended 1997]) : in Category 1 Dogs bred for fighting,for example, the Pit Bull terrier, Fila Brasileiro, Japanese Tosa and Argentine dogo, as well as any dog 'bred for fighting or to have the characteristics of a type bred for that purpose' ; and guard dogs, such as the Rottweiler, Staffordshire terrier and Mastiff breeds, and dogs 'bred to have the characteristics of a type bred for that purpose'. Some insurers will not insure racing dogs either.

⊕ Generally included in the insurance are:

The reimbursement of **medical expenses** in the case of an accident or illness, and these normally include the following:
- Vet's fees
- Prescribed medicines

- Costs of any medical tests and examinations
- Costs of transport in an animal ambulance, if necessary.

Reimbursement of fees for a **surgical operation** in the case of an accident or illness, i.e.:
- Specific fees for the surgical operation
- The costs of drugs, anaesthetic and care directly linked to the surgical operation
- The costs of hospitalisation in a veterinary clinic necessitated by surgery.

Certain insurance companies will also reimburse the expenses incurred in boarding the dog in a kennel if the owner is himself hospitalised, as well as a part of or the whole of the annual costs related to the dog's vaccinations.

The amounts reimbursed vary considerably from one insurance company to another. It can go from 50 to 100 per cent of the real costs incurred and may or may not be subject to payment of an excess, i.e. a minimum sum which in each case will be down to the owner to pay. Certain companies also impose a ceiling on how much they will pay up, i.e. a maximum sum for a certain period of insurance (generally one year) for the same dog, or the same condition, so once this limit has been reached, the owner can no longer be reimbursed, even if the animal needs further care.

⊕ **Generally excluded from the insurance are:**
- Any accidents intentionally caused or provoked by the insured or with his complicity
- The consequences of ill-treatment such as kicks, lack of care, food deprivation
- Wounds resulting from organised fights
- Treatment which has not been carried out by a registered vet
- Cosmetic operations, such as ear cropping, tail docking

- Expenses incurred by illness which could have been prevented if vaccinations had been done
- Expenses connected with malformations, whether they are hereditary or not (hip dysplasia, patellar luxation, testicular ectopion, teeth anomalies; eye anomalies)
- The consequence of accidents or illnesses which occurred prior to signature of the contract

🐕 **It is very important to read the small print extremely carefully, especially the paragraph concerning exclusions as these vary considerably from one company to another.**

⊕ **A no claims bonus/surcharge:** Similar to car insurance, a few companies have now adopted this practice. If the dog's owner has not needed to call upon his insurers in the preceding year he will pay a smaller new premium, while if he has had to call upon the insurers to pay out several times in the preceding year, he will be penalised with a surcharge the next time he pays his premium.

🐕 **The premiums vary according to where you live in the UK, the size and breed of your dog, whether it has been identichipped, what security arrangements you have at home, whether or not you have other dogs. Besides vet's fees, the policy can cover many things, among them third party liability, recovery expenses, boarding fees, expenses incurred in finding a lost or stolen dog, accidental damage, holiday cancellation, overseas travel cover, quarantine costs, emergency expenses cover abroad, even your animal's death from an accident or illness. Companies often also provide different levels of insurance: Bronze, Silver, Gold Platinum, or Essential and Super, but in general you get what you pay for, so it is not always advisable to plump for the cheapest option. There are currently over 260 companies in the UK that offer pet insurance.**

Short glossary of the most common pathologies found in elderly dogs

Abscess Swelling due to an accumulation of pus in a natural cavity or formed by the pus itself

Acidosis Pathological condition of the blood characterised by an acid reaction, especially in cases of severe diabetes or poisoning

Acute oedema of the lungs A very serious manifestation of respiratory insufficiency provoked by the invasion of blood serum into the lungs

Adenoma Benign tumour

Alkalosis Pathological condition of the blood characterised by an excessive level of alkalinity

Alopecia Localised or general loss of hair, baldness

Amyloidosis Deposit of an amorphous substance (amyloid) in organs hindering their proper functioning

Anaemia Decrease in the number of red corpuscles in the blood

Arthritis Inflammation of a joint

Asthma Respiratory anomaly originating in an allergy and due to a spasm of the bronchial tubes

Ataxia Problems with balance, when standing or walking. Poor coordination of voluntary movements

Balanitis Inflammation of the glans penis

Balanopostitis Inflammation of the glans penis and sheath

Bradycardia Abnormally low rate of heart beat

Chronic bronchitis Inflammation of the bronchial tubes due to irritation and infections

Cachexia Condition of extreme thinness/ weakness resulting from any chronic debilitating illness

Carcinoma Cancerous tumour

Cataract Opacification of the crystalline lens of the eye

Cholecystitis Inflammation of the gall bladder

Cirrhosis Hepatic degeneration (cancer of the liver)

Colitis Inflammation of the colon

Corneal dystrophy A nutritional problem of the cornea

Cranio-mandibular osteopathy Bone disease which manifests itself in an irregular proliferation of bone in the lower jaw (mandible) and the tympanic bulla

Cushing's syndrome Illness connected to the dysfunction of the adrenal glands, manifested by a pendulous abdomen and hair loss (this can occur after cortisone injections)

Cyanosis Bluish or purplish colouring of mucous revealing a lack of oxygenation of the blood

Cystitis Inflammation of the internal mucous of the bladder (the animal wants to urinate all the time)

Dermatitis Inflammation of the dermis (i.e. the skin)

Demodectic mange Cutaneous infection caused by an acarid or parasitic mite, *demodex canis*

Diabetes insipidus Form of diabetes causing excessive thirst and excretion of large quantities of dilute urine

Diabetes mellitus Increase in the level of glucose in the blood

Discal disease Anomaly of the position of the intervertebral discs (slipped discs) which can lead to a depression of the spinal marrow which in turn will lead to a weakening of the muscles or paralysis

Dyslipidemia Anomaly in the level of lipids in the blood

Ectopic ureter Incorrect positioning of the ureter (the duct which links the kidney to the bladder)

Ectropion The eyelid droops away from the eye and does not cover it properly

Embolism Obstruction of a blood vessel by a clot

Encephalitis Disease of the central nervous system (brain, cerebellum and medulla oblongata)

Enteritis Inflammation of the intestinal mucous which manifests itself as diarrhoea or constipation

Entropion Inwardly turned eyelid

Enuresis Nocturnal incontinence

Epilepsy Attacks of convulsions with loss of consciousness

Extrasystoles Early contractions of the auricles and ventricles of the heart

Faecalomia Accumulation of faecal matter in a part of the intestine

Fibroid Benign tumour made of fibrous tissue

Foliaceous emphigus Disease of the immune system leading to numerous skin problems, such as loss of hair, lesions in the dermis, lesions in the paw pads

Gastritis Inflammation of the mucosa in the stomach, causing vomiting

Gastro-enteritis An inflammation of the stomach and intestinal mucosa, often caused by a virus, and causing vomiting and diarrhoea

Glaucoma Increase in the pressure of intra-ocular fluid
Glomerulonephritis Inflammation of the kidney

Haematoma Pocket of blood in a natural cavity or under the skin caused by the rupture of internal vessels
Haematuria Presence of blood in the urine (giving it a red colour)
Haemophilia Disease of the blood causing spontaneous haemorrhaging and prolonged bleeding
Hepatitis Inflammation of the liver that can originate in an infection or poisoning
Hernia The case when part of an organ pops out of its original natural cavity
Hip dysplasia Congenital and hereditary bone disease which causes a poor fit between the head of the femur and the joint cavity of the pelvis which is there to accommodate it
Histiocytoma Small cutaneous tumour, round in shape and of connective tissue in origin
Hypothyroid Insufficiency of the secretion of thyroid hormones

I

Icterus Yellow colouring of mucous membranes and skin due to jaundice
Ictus A stroke. This is manifested in a loss of activity in one part of the brain and can cause paralysis down one side of the body
Impetigo Contagious skin infection due to the presence of staphylococci or streptococci
Intestinal obstruction Abnormal stoppage (due to the closure of a duct) of food matter in the intestines

Keratitis Inflammation causing the cornea of the eye to become opaque

Laryngitis Inflammation of the larynx which causes a strong loud coughing

Legg-Calvé-Perthes disease Aseptic necrosis of the head of the femur, frequently found in small breeds, leading to lameness and the destruction of the head of the femur

Lens luxation Displacement of the crystalline lens of the eye due to the weakness of the ligaments holding it in place

Leptospirosis This is canine typhus, caused by a germ called leptospirus (also known as Weil's disease)

Leukocytosis Abnormal increase in the number of white corpuscles

Lipofuschinosis Accumulation of pigments called lipofuscins in the nervous system, leading to behavioural problems

Luxation Displacement of the two parts of a joint

Luxation of the eyeball When the eyeball comes out of its socket

Macroglossia An abnormally large tongue

Mange Parasitic skin infection caused by acarids

Mastitis Breast or udder infection

Mastosis Mammary adenoma with the formation of cysts

Meningitis Inflammation of the meninges (the membranes that surround the brain and spinal cord) caused by a viral, toxic or mycotic (fungal) infection

Metritis Acute or chronic inflammation of the uterus

Microphthalmia Abnormal development of the eyes, which remain too small

Mycosis Infection caused by parasitic fungi

Myelopathy Infection of the bone marrow leading to nervous and loco-motor problems

Myocarditis Inflammation of the heart muscle (myocardia)

Myotonia Muscular infection causing an exaggerated slowness of decontraction

Necrosis Physico-chemical transformation that living matter under-goes, ending in death

Nephritis Inflammatory disease of the kidney, frequently found in old dogs

Oedema Swelling of subcutaneous tissue or of an organ with the infil-tration of serous liquid

Optic neuritis Inflammatory lesions of the optic nerve

Osteitis Inflammation of bone tissue

Osteoarthritis Premature ageing of joints, leading to progressive destruction of the cartilage, often associated with osteophytes (small abnormal bony outgrowths)

Otitis Inflammation of the ear

Pancreatic insufficiency Anomaly or absence of secretions from the pancreas which often causes the dog to get thin

Pancreatitis Inflammation of the pancreas

Parvo virus enteritis Gastro-enteritis caused by the parvo virus, which is particularly serious if it affects puppies or elderly dogs

Peritonitis Inflammation of the serous membrane which lines the abdomen

Phlebitis Inflammation of a vein which can result in the formation of a blood clot and thence the risk of an embolism

Piroplasmosis Infection of the red blood corpuscles transmitted to the dog through ticks (very deep colour of the urine)

Polyneuropathy Infection of the nerves causing lameness and a progressive weakening of the muscles

Porto-systemic shunt Anomaly in the development of certain vessels, especially the hepatic vessels which can lead to blood poisoning

Progressive retinal atrophy Defective vision, first at night then in daytime, resulting in complete blindness

Prostatitis Inflammation of the prostate, very common in elderly dogs

Pulmonary emphysema Permanent dilation of the pulmonary alveoli, which causes breathlessness and a dry cough

Pulmonary stenosis Stricture of the pulmonary artery

Pyometra Pocketing of pus inside the uterus

Rectitis Inflammation of the rectum

Renal cortical hypoplasia Disease of the external layer of the kidney causing polydipsia and polyuria (the dog drinks and pees much too much)

Renal hypoplasia Abnormally small kidney

Rhinitis Inflammation of nasal mucous

Sarcoma Cancerous tumour of the connective tissues

Septicaemia Blood poisoning caused by the presence of numerous germs

Stomatitis Inflammation of oral mucosa

Syringomyelia Destruction of the grey matter of the spinal cord, which can lead to a loss of sensitivity (stricture of spinal cord)

Tachycardia Acceleration of the heart beat

Thrombocytopaenia Abnormal diminution of the number of blood platelets

Thrombosis Formation of a blood clot in a blood vessel or in a vascular cavity

Tracheitis Inflammation of the trachea

Ulcer Indicates a hole formed by the loss of matter in a tissue

Uraemia Abnormal increase in the amount of urea (nitrogenous matter eliminated in urine) in the blood

Vaginitis Inflammation of the vagina

Vulvitis Inflammation of the vulva

Zoonosis Said of a disease that is transmittable from an animal to a human and vice-versa

Useful addresses

My address?
I live with my dogs at villa de la Capponcina.

GABRIELE D'ANNUNZIO

BREED CLUBS AND SOCIETIES

The following is a small selection. For a full list of regional societies and clubs, you can refer to *The Kennel Club Yearbook.*

⊕ Hounds

AFGHAN HOUND ASSOCIATION, BS
Mrs G Link, 19 Stonehouse Road, Bromsgrove, Worcs B60 2JY.
Tel. 01527 871061

BASENJI CLUB OF GREAT BRITAIN, BS
Mr S Bell, 'Holmeswood', Main Street, Old Weston, Huntingdon, Cambridgeshire PE28 5LL.
Tel: 01832 293422

BASSET HOUND CLUB, BS
Mrs J Scott-Goldstone, Flat 3, 10 Boyne Park, Tunbridge Wells, Kent TN4 8ET.
Tel: 01892 531156. Email: riscottgoldstone@aol.com. Web: www.bassethoundclub.co.uk

BEAGLE ASSOCIATION, BS
Miss S Kimber, 5 The Beeches, Sole Street, Gravesend, Kent DA13 9BT.
Tel: 0845 456 8334. Email: beagle.assoc@btinternet.com.
Web: beagleassociation.btinternet.co.uk

BLOODHOUND CLUB, BS, WT
Mrs E Richards, Pond Farm, Vines Cross, Heathfield, Sussex TN21 9AR.
Tel: 01435 862455

BORZOI CLUB, BS
Mrs C Spencer, Willow Pool, Toll Bar Cross, Chulmleigh, Devon EX18 7AF.
Tel: 01769 580578

DACHSHUND CLUB, BS
Mrs A Moore, Hill Farm, Willesley Woodside, Willesley, Ashby-de-la-Zouch, Leics LE65 2UP.
Tel: 01530 271796

LONGHAIRED DACHSHUND CLUB, BS
Mr T M Watkins, 37 New Road, Croxley Green, Rickmansworth, Herts WD3 3EN.
Tel: 01923 896934. Email: LHDCtrevorw@aol.com. Web: www.longhaired-dachsundclub.co.uk

MINIATURE DACHSHUND CLUB, BS
Mrs W Spencer, The Old Pump House, Forest Road, Long Street, Hanslope, Bucks MK19 7DE.
Tel: 01908 510796

SMOOTH HAIRED DACHSHUND CLUB, BS
Mrs R A Rawson, 'Hilltops', Ratten Row, Langtoft, Driffield, E Yorks YO25 3TJ.
Tel: 01377 267344

WIREHAIRED DACHSHUND CLUB, BS
Mrs L Sexton, 8 Victoria Bungalows, Old Maidstone Road, Upper Ruxley, Sidcup, Kent DA14 5BA.
Tel: 0208 302 5919

DEERHOUND CLUB, BS
Miss M Girling, Lodge Farm, Brightlingsea, Nr Colchester, Essex CO7 0QJ.
Tel: 01206 302072

GREYHOUND CLUB, BS
Miss C Boggia, Cedar Croft, Graveney, Faversham,
Kent ME13 9EF.
Tel: 01795 535719

IRISH WOLFHOUND CLUB, BS, CZ
Mr D Malley, Ainsaa Cottage, Chapel Lane,
Holmeswood, Lancashire L40 1UD.
Tel: 01704 823532

IRISH WOLFHOUND CLUB OF NORTHERN IRELAND
BS
Mrs M A Finney, Gulliagh House, Baldurgan Hill,
Ballyboughal, Co Dublin, Ireland.
Tel: 00353 18078993

RHODESIAN RIDGEBACK CLUB OF GREAT BRITAIN,
BS, CZ
Mrs K Maidment, The Old Granary, Water
Stratford Road, Finmere, Bucks MK18 4AT.
Tel: 01280 847164

RHODESIAN RIDGEBACK CLUB OF SCOTLAND, BS,
CZ
Mr R Mason, Middle Third House, Newton Of
Pitcairns, Dunning, Perth PH2 0RE.
Tel: 01764 684021

SALUKI OR GAZELLE HOUND CLUB, BS
Dr J Hudson, 28 Cootes Lane, Fen Drayton,
Cambridge CB4 5SL
Tel: 01954 203084

SLOUGHI CLUB; BS, CZ
Mrs M Goodman, 34 Bridge Street, Leominster,
Hereford HR6 8DX
Tel: 01568 611609

NATIONAL WHIPPET ASSOCIATION, BS
Mrs M Blanks, 36 New Waverley Road, Laindon,
Basildon, Essex SS15 4BH.
Tel: 01268 288091

⊕ **Gundogs**

BRACCO ITALIANO SOCIETY (PROVISIONAL), BS
Mrs C Dewar, 63 Swallowdale, Iver Heath, Bucks
SL0 0EX.
Tel: 01753 655217

BRITTANY CLUB OF GREAT BRITAIN, BS, FT4
Mrs J Robinson, 1 Brimington Road, Willerby, Hull
HU10 6JU.
Tel: 01482 651614

ENGLISH SETTER ASSOCIATION, BS
Mr R E Evans, Briar Cottage, Plump Hill,
Mitcheldean, Glos GL17 0ET.
Tel: 01594 544190

ENGLISH SETTER CLUB, BS, FT3
Mr M Daw, Springfield, Sigingstone, Cowbridge,
South Glamorgan, Wales CF71 7LP.
Tel: 01446 772973

ENGLISH SETTER SOCIETY OF SCOTLAND, BS
Mrs C Normansell, 54 James Street, Alva,
Clackmannanshire FK12 5AJ.
Tel: 01259 760866

IRISH RED & WHITE SETTER CLUB OF GREAT
BRITAIN, BS, CZ
Mrs S A Barry, 1 Cherry Tree Cottages,
Wethersfield Road, Sible Hedingham, Halstead,
Essex CO9 3LZ.
Tel: 01787 461339

BELFAST & DISTRICT IRISH SETTER CLUB, BS
Mrs D Park, 'Ladysdale', 103 Oldstone Road,
Antrim, N Ireland BT41 4SP.
Tel: 02894 467961

IRISH SETTER ASSOCIATION, ENGLAND, BS, CZ,
FT3
Mrs P Cowell, 9 Bromsgrove Road, Hagley,
Stourbridge, West Midlands DY9 9LY.
Tel: 01562 882013

IRISH SETTER CLUB OF SCOTLAND, BS, CZ
Mr B M Marshall, 27 Raith Drive, Kirkcaldy, Fife
KY2 5NW.
Tel: 01592 260275

IRISH SETTER CLUB OF WALES, BS
Mr P Rowlands, 11 Ffordd Lerry, Wrexham, Clwyd
LL12 8JB.
Tel: 01978 357393

POINTER CLUB, BS, FT3
Mrs A Howes, Mandarin, Henley Road, Nuneham
Courtenay, Oxford OX44 9PR.
Tel: 01865 343435

GOLDEN RETRIEVER CLUB, BS, FT1
Gp Capt R B Bridges, Durridge House, Kerswell
Green, Kempsey, Worcs WR5 3PE.
Tel: 01905 371315

LABRADOR RETRIEVER CLUB, BS, FT]
Mr A Ellis, Llwyn, Llanystumdwy, Cricieth,
Gwynedd, N Wales LL52 0ST.
Tel: 01766 522146

CLUMBER SPANIEL CLUB, BS, CZ, FT
Mrs C Page, 'Micklemess', 20 Swanwick Lane,
Swanwick, Southampton SO31 7HF.
Tel: 01489 589734

COCKER SPANIEL CLUB, BS, FT2
Mrs A Webster, Lilac Cottage, Cliffe Hill, Stanton
under Bardon, Marksfield LE67 9TE.
Tel: 01530 249952

PARTI-COLOURED COCKER SPANIEL CLUB, BS
Mrs C Steeples, 210 Leicester Road, Markfield,
Leicester LE67 9RF.
Tel 01530 244260

SOLID COLOURS COCKER SPANIEL ASSOCIATION,
BS
Miss S Kettle, Marvay Southend Road,
Corringham, Essex SS17 9ET.
Tel: 01268 554619

ENGLISH SPRINGER SPANIEL CLUB, BS, FT2
Ms Y Billows, Pine Crest, Chester Road, Oakmere,
Cheshire CW8 2HB.
Tel: 01606 888 303

ENGLISH SPRINGER SPANIEL CLUB OF NORTHERN
IRELAND, BS, FT2
Mr M Stewart, 8 Liscloon Drive, Derry, Co
Londonderry, Northern Ireland BT48 8HS

ENGLISH SPRINGER SPANIEL CLUB OF WALES, BS,
FT2
Mr W Lewis, 21 Ffordd Emlyn Ystlyfera, Swansea
SA9 2EW.
Tel: 01639 844355. Email:
wayne@lewisw.fslife.co.uk

ENGLISH SPRINGER SPANIEL CLUB OF SCOTLAND,
BS, FT2
Mr G Ford, Hillswick, Abercromby Road, Castle
Douglas DG7 IBA.
Tel: 01556 502430

WEIMARANER ASSOCIATION, BS, FT4
Mrs A Harris, The Gables, 54A Priory Road,
Peterborough, Cambs PE3 9ED.
Tel: 01733 566927. Web: www.weimaraner-
association.org.uk

⊕ Terriers

NATIONAL AIREDALE TERRIER ASSOCIATION, BS
Mrs R Moules, The Chimneys, 1 Glebe Cottage,
Hougham, Grantham, Lincs NG32 2JG.
Tel: 01400 250969

BEDLINGTON TERRIER ASSOCIATION, BS
Mrs V Rainsbury, 174 Bells Road, Gorleston On
Sea, Gt Yarmouth, Norfolk NR31 6BA.
Tel: 01493 440972. Email: viv@thebta.co.uk.
Web: www.thebta.co.uk

BORDER TERRIER CLUB, BS
Mrs K Wilkinson, Peel House, Edmondsley,
Durham DH7 6DL.
Tel: 0191 3719405. Email: otterkin@aol.com

BULL TERRIER CLUB, BS
Mrs P Rawlings, The Old Police House, Main Street,
Lubenham, Market Harborough, Leicestershire LE16
9TG.
Tel: 01858 432610

MINIATURE BULL TERRIER CLUB, BS
Mrs M Barrett, 26 Low Road, Dewsbury Moor,
Dewsbury, West Yorkshire WF13 3PP.
Tel: 01924 502141

CAIRN TERRIER ASSOCIATION, BS
Mrs C Butterfield, 27 Settrington, Malton, N Yorks
YO17 8NP.
Tel: 01944 768357

DANDIE DINMONT TERRIER CLUB, BS
Mrs A Harpwood, Finloren Cottage, Weythel, Old
Radnor, Powys LD8 2RR.
Tel: 01544 370213. Email:
treasurer@ddtc.co.uk. Web: www.ddtc.co.uk

FOX TERRIER CLUB, BS
Mrs S Wiggins, 226 Cradley Road, Netherton,
Dudley, W. Midlands DY2 9TE.
Tel. 01384 567490

SMOOTH FOX TERRIER ASSOCIATION, BS
Mrs R Turner, Plas Llewelyn, Y Fron, Upper
Llandwrog Gwynedd LL54 7BG.
Tel: 01286 881344

WIRE FOX TERRIER ASSOCIATION, BS
Mrs B Kay, Riverwood, Brandon Road, Thetford,
Norfolk IP24 3ND.
Tel: 01842 754791

IRISH TERRIER ASSOCIATION, BS
Miss A Bradley, Swans Reach, 170 Glassmore Bank
Road, Whittlesey, Peterborough, Cambridgeshire PE7
2LT.
Tel: 01733 205386

ULSTER IRISH TERRIER CLUB, BS
Mrs B Dorrian, 10d Cross Lane, Magheragall,
Lisburn, Co Antrim BT28 2TH.
Tel: 028 92 621972

KERRY BLUE TERRIER ASSOCIATION, BS, CZ
Ms P Munro, 'Rose Cottage', Mill Lane,
Pebmarsh, Essex CO9 2NW.
Tel: 01787 269977

KERRY BLUE TERRIER ASSOCIATION OF NORTHERN IRELAND, BS
Mr J G Keery, 4 Maze View Road, Listullycurran, Dromore, Co Down, Northern Ireland BT25 1RE
Tel: 028 92 692866

LAKELAND TERRIER CLUB, BS
Mrs K Peake, Park Cottage, Widecombe in the Moor, Newton Abbot, Devon TQ13 7TR.
Tel: 01364 621287

LAKELAND TERRIER SOCIETY, BS
Mrs J Patterson, Eikal House, 1 Kersland Road, Glengarnock, Ayrshire, Scotland KA14 3BA.
Tel: 01505 682680

NORFOLK TERRIER CLUB OF GREAT BRITAIN, BS, CZ
Mr I Mackison, Farm Cottage, 11 High Street, Weedon, Aylesbury, Bucks HP22 4NW.
Tel: 01296 641269. Email: jmackison.weedon@btinternet.com. Web: www.norfolkterrierclub.co.uk

NORWICH TERRIER CLUB, BS
Ms G Bardell, Acquest House, 50 Priory Road, Campton, Bedfordshire SG17 5PG.
Tel: 01462 814412

PARSON RUSSELL TERRIER CLUB, BS, CZ
Mrs R M Hussey Wilford, Pirton House, Pirton, Worcester WR8 9EJ.
Tel: 01905 821440

SCOTTISH TERRIER CLUB (ENGLAND), BS
Mrs I Tovey, 2 Dalgleish Way, Asfordby, Melton Mowbray, Leicestershire LE14 3RX.
Tel: 01664 813179

SCOTTISH TERRIER CLUB (SCOTLAND), BS
Mrs M Plunkett, 2 Smiths Croft, Auldgirth, Dumfries DG2 0XG.
Tel: 01387 740420

SEALYHAM TERRIER BREEDERS ASSOCIATION, BS
Mr D Winsley, 220A Hurn Road, Matchams, Ringwood, Hants BH24 2BT.
Tel. 01425 479013

SEALYHAM TERRIER CLUB, BS
Mrs J Wonnacott, Headlands, South Hook Road, Gelliswick Bay, Milford Haven, Pembrokeshire SA73 3RU.
Tel: 01646 698786

SKYE TERRIER CLUB, BS
Mr M Taylor, Westlea, Kyleakin, Isle of Skye IV41 8PH
Tel: 01599 534391

STAFFORDSHIRE BULL TERRIER CLUB, BS
Mr J F Beaufoy, Wyrefare Cottage, Yew Tree Lane, Bewdley, Worcestershire DY12 2PJ
Tel: 01299 403382. Email: jbeaufoy@aol.com. Web: www.thesbtc.com

WELSH TERRIER ASSOCIATION, BS
Mrs N Evans, Ty-Segur-Bach, Eaglesbush Valley, Neath, West Glam SA11 2AN.
Tel: 01639 636509

WEST HIGHLAND WHITE TERRIER CLUB, BS
Mrs B Wilson, Castleton Farm, Kiiwinning, Ayrshire KA13 7QH.
Tel: 01294 557259

⊕ Utility

BOSTON TERRIER CLUB BS
Mrs V Tanner, Thaika, Blackness Road,
Crowborough, E Sussex TN6 2NB.
Tel: 01892 652095

BRITISH BULLDOG CLUB, BS
Ms E Aldridge, Shepherds Bush Farm, Main Road,
Long Bennington, Newark, Notts NG23 5EB.
Tel: 01400 282163

CHINESE CHOW CLUB, BS
Mrs M Bennett, Matapos, 67 Lodge Close, Stoke
D'Abernon, Cobham, Surrey KT11 2SQ.
Tel: 01932 862304

CHOW CHOW CLUB, BS
Mrs V Elsworth, 'Miyun', 7 Drove Road,
Biggleswade, Bedfordshire SG18 8HD.
Tel: 01767 313163

BRITISH DALMATIAN CLUB, BS, CZ
Mrs S Stevenson, Hanch Cottage, Lysways Lane,
Lichfield, Staffs WS13 8HQ.
Tel: 01543 490849

DALMATIAN CLUB OF SCOTLAND, BS
Mrs C Whyte, Mansefield, Glebe Road, Kilbirnie,
Ayrshire KA25 6HX.
Tel: 01505 683402

FRENCH BULLDOG CLUB OF ENGLAND, BS
Mrs P Rankine-Parsons, 18 High Street.
Robertsbridge, E Sussex TN32 5AE.
Tel: 01580 881043

GERMAN SPITZ CLUB, BS, CZ
Mrs V A Dyer, Waterend Cottage, Hayes End,
Longney, Gloucester GL2 3SW.
Tel: 01452 720594

JAPANESE SPITZ CLUB, BS
Mrs J Moody, 46 Hanbury Close, Burnham, Bucks
SL1 7EA.
Tel: 01628 548813

KEESHOND CLUB, BS
Mr B Bennett, Kenton House, Main Road,
Stickney, Boston, Lincolnshire PE22 8EF
Tel: 01205 480154

LHASO APSO CLUB, BS
Mr G Holmes, 39 St Edmunds Rise, Taverham,
Norwich, Norfolk NR8 6PA.
Tel: 01603 868280

MINIATURE SCHNAUZER CLUB, BS, CZ
Mrs S P McGrann, The Grange, Ewerby Waithe,
Sleaford, Lincs NG34 9PS.
Tel: 01526 860087

POODLE CLUB, BS
Mr & Mrs N E Butcher, Tinoth Lodge, Lambourne
End, N Romford, Essex RM4 1NA.
Tel: 020 8500 2335

MINIATURE POODLE CLUB, BS
Miss J Kitchener, Milburn, 11 New Road, Langtoft,
Peterborough PE6 9LE.
Tel: 01778 348106

BRITISH TOY POODLE CLUB, BS
Mr L Harwood, 7 Dane End Road, Westgate On
Sea, Kent CT8 8PH.
Tel: 01843 833631

SCHIPPERKE CLUB, BS
Mrs J Holland, Benthow, Lowca, Whitehaven,
Cumbria CA28 6QT.
Tel: 01946 832804. Email.
Schojan@compuserve.com

SCHNAUZER CLUB OF GREAT BRITAIN, BS, CZ
Mrs M Gill, Sunnyside, 84 Molrams Lane, Great
Baddow, Chelmsford, Essex CM2 7AJ.
Tel: 01245 475441

SHAR-PEI CLUB OF GREAT BRITAIN, BS, CZ
Mr V Rodger, 31 Chilside Road, Felling,
Gateshead, Tyne & Wear NE10 9DY.
Tel: 0191 4384505. Web: www.spcgb.co.uk

SHIH TZU CLUB, BS, CZ
Mrs P Gregory, Marpalyn, 5 Radnor Park, Corston,
Nr Malmesbury, Wiltshire SN16 ONE.
Tel: 01666 822380

TIBETAN SPANIEL ASSOCIATION, BS
Miss B Croucher, 5 Uplands Crescent, Uplands,
Swansca, West Glamorgan SA2 0BA.
Tel: 01792 470417

TIBETAN TERRIER ASSOCIATION, BS, CZ
Ms C Sayer, 6 Burlington Rise, East Barnet, Herts
EN4 8NN.
Tel: 020 8361 2540. Email: thesecretary@the-
tta.org.uk Web: www.the-tta.org.uk

TIBETAN TERRIER BREEDERS & OWNERS CLUB, BS
Mrs P Gilbert, Chiltern Cottage, Frith Hill, Great
Missenden, Bucks HP16 9QF.
Tel: 01494 867266

⊕ **Working dogs**

ALASKAN MALAMUTE CLUB OF THE UNITED KING-
DOM, BS, CZ
Mrs J Broadberry, Orchard Wood, Winkburn,
Newark, Notts NG22 8PN.
Tel: 01636 636660

BERNESE MOUNTAIN DOG CLUB OF GREAT
BRITAIN, BS, CZ
Mrs J Green, The Lodge, 1 Kirkby Road, Desford,
Leicester LE9 9GL

BOUVIER DES FLANDRES CLUB OF GREAT BRITAIN,
BS, CZ
Mrs J Laing, Grange Bungalow, Chapel Lane,
Hardwick, Norwich NR15 2SW.
Tel: 01508 531614

BRITISH BOXER CLUB, BS, TC, CZ
Mrs M Seeney, Winnaway Kennels, The
Winnaway, Harwell, Oxford OX11 0JQ.
Tel: 01235 835207

BULLMASTIFF ASSOCIATION, BS
Mrs L Bedson, 'Brinscall', Fulford Manor, Fulford,
Stoke on Trent, Staffs ST11 9QR.
Tel: 01782 393251

DOBERMANN CLUB, BS, CZ
Mrs V M Lucas, Malden Cottage, Green Lane,
Fenhouses, Swineshead, Boston, Lincs PE20 3HN.
Tel: 01205 821583

DOGUE DE BORDEAUX CLU8 OF GREAT BRITAIN
(PROVISIONAL), BS
Mr A Bicknell, Corvet Wood, 120 Redehall Road,
Smallfield, Surrey RH6 9RS.
Tel: 01342 842705

GERMAN PINSCHER CLUB, BS
Mrs G Cuthbert 'Oak Ridge', 87 London Road,
Liphook, Hampshire GU30 7SG
Tel: 01428 727115 Email:
frank.cuthbert@dsl.pipex.com

GIANT SCHNAUZER CLUB, BS, CZ
Mrs K Carroll, 248 Oxcliffe Road, Morecombe,
Lancs LA3 3EH.
Tel: 01524 411220

GREAT DANE BREEDERS' & OWNERS ASSOCIA-
TION, BS
Mrs M Stevens, Highfield, Longfield Avenue,
Longfield, Kent DA3 7LA.
Tel: 01474 703470

GREAT DANE CLUB, BS
Mrs M Hipkin, Rose Cottage, Tilbury Road, Great
Yeldham, Halstead, Essex CO9 4JG.
Tel: 01787 237969

GREENLAND DOG CLUB OF GREAT BRITAIN, BS
Mrs P Phillips, Cockett Farm, Ferryhill, Basford, Nr
Leek, Staffordshire ST13 7ET.
Tel: 01538 361110

LEONBERGER CLUB OF GREAT BRITAIN, BS, CZ
Mrs S Sevastopulo, Highbridge Farm, Dymock
Road, Ledbury, Herefordshire HR8 2HT.
Tel: 01531 632798. Email:
oldholbans@tiscali.co.uk Web: www.leonberger-
club.co.uk

MASTIFF ASSOCIATION, BS
Mr R Benfield, 6 Trent Road, Cannock, Staffs
WS11 2QZ.
Tel: 01543 876504

OLD ENGLISH MASTIFF CLUB, BS
Mrs J Atkinson, 'The Bungalow', Fisherman's
Lane, Aldermarston, Berkshire RG7 4LL.
Tel: 01189 712124. Email: oemc@btopen-
world.com. Web: www.mastiffclub.com

NEAPOLITAN MASTIFF CLUB, BS
Mrs K South, The Sabres, High Road, Laindon,
Essex SS15 6DB.
Tel: 01268 455791

NEWFOUNDLAND CLUB, BS, CZ
Mrs M Pitcher, Conifers, 31 Pipwell Gate, Moulton
Seas End, Spalding, Lincs PE12 6LU.
Tel: 01406 371477

PYRENEAN MASTIFF ASSOCIATION OF THE UK
(PROVISIONAL), BS
Mrs M Dunk, 1 Emscote Road, Lower Stoke,
Coventry, West Midlands CV3 IHF.
Tel: 02476 447591

BRITISH ROTTWEILER ASSOCIATION, BS, CZ
Mrs M Yates, 1 Albansfield, People Street,
Wymondham, Norfolk NR18 OPR.
Tel: 01953 600602

ROTTWEILER CLUB, BS, CZ
Mrs M Fletcher, Woodlands, Top Road, Osgodby,
Lincolnshire LN8 3TG.
Tel: 01673 843640

SIBERIAN HUSKY CLUB OF GREAT BRITAIN, BS
Mrs P Evans, 45 Deacon Place, Middleton, Milton
Keynes, Bucks MK10 9FS.
Tel: 01908 609796

ENGLISH ST BERNARD CLUB, BS, CZ
Mrs L Martin, The Paddocks, Brinkworth (west
end), Nr Chippenham, Wilts SN15 5DA.
Tel: 01666 510295

ST BERNARD CLUB OF SCOTLAND, BS
Mr M McMenemy, 7 Orr Street, St Paisley,
Scotland PA2 6LT.
Tel: 0141 889 9825

TIBETAN MASTIFF CLUB OF GREAT BRITAIN, BS
Mrs I Feddon, 157 Green Lane, New Eltham,
London SE9 35Y.
Tel: 020 8859 1309

⊕ Pastoral

ANATOLIAN SHEPHERD DOG CLUB OF GREAT
BRITAIN, BS
Miss A Grove, The Cottage, Lower Cargenwen,
Black Rock, Praze-an-Beeble, Camborne, Cornwall
TR14 9PJ
Tel: 01209 831921

BEARDED COLLIE CLUB, BS, CZ, AG
Mrs Y Fox, Peters Bank Cottage, Harperley
Stanley, Co Durham DH9 9TY.
Tel: 01207 290036

BELGIAN SHEPHERD DOG ASSOCIATION OF GREAT
BRITAIN, BS, CZ
Dr M Pratten, 'Concord', 145 Belper Road,
Stanley Common, Derbyshire DE7 6FT.
Tel: 0115 9448145

BERGAMASCO CLUB OF GREAT BRITAIN (PROVI-
SIONAL), BS, CZ
Mr S Band, 2 Elsmere Cottages, Priory Road,
Ascot, Berks SL5 8DY.
Tel: 01344 884137

BORDER COLLIE CLUB OF GREAT BRITAIN, BS, CZ,
AG
Mr J Collins, 257 Councillor Lane, Cheadle,
Stockport, Cheshire SK8 5PN.
Tel: 0161 485 4544

BORDER COLLIE CLUB OF WALES, BS, TC, CZ, AG
Mr G Clarke 16 Whitley Close, Middlewich,
Cheshire CW10 0NQ.
Tel: 01606 738078

BRIARD (BERGER DE BRIE) ASSOCIATION, BS, CZ
Mrs L Webb, Bridge House, Eaugate Road,
Moulton Eaugate, Spalding, Lincolnshire PE12
0XJ.
Tel: 01406 380611

COLLIE ASSOCIATION, BS, CZ
Mrs C Smedley, Brook Cottage, Ripley,
Christchurch, Dorset BH23 8EU.
Tel: 01425 672424

SMOOTH COLLIE CLUB OF GREAT BRITAIN, BS, CZ
Mrs M Foulston, 22 Sycamore Drive, Elm Park,
Hixon, Staffs ST18 0FB.
Tel: 01998 271053

GERMAN SHEPHERD DOG (ALSATIAN) CLUB OF
THE UNITED KINGDOM, BS, CZ
Miss J Hassall, 41 Bawtry Road, Harworth,
Doncaster DN11 8PA.
Tel: 01302 751743

GERMAN SHEPHERD DOG CLUB OF NORTHERN
IRELAND, BS
Mr A Balmer, 37 Ballymacvea, Shanksbridge, Co
Antrim, Northern Ireland BT42 3NQ.
Tel: 02825 892477

GERMAN SHEPHERD DOG CLUB OF SCOTLAND, BS
Mrs E Young, Glenview Cottage, Tarholm,
Auchinchruive By Ayr KA6 5HY.
Tel: 0292 521129

MAREMMA SHEEPDOG CLUB OF GREAT BRITAIN,
BS
Mrs C Walsh, Needhams Farm, Uplands Road,
Werneth Low, Gee Cross, Nr Hyde, Cheshire SK14
3AG.
Tel: 0161 368 4610

OLD ENGLISH SHEEPDOG CLUB, BS
Mrs P Barnes, South Farm House, Ypres Road,
Chisledon, Nr Swindon, Wilts SN4 OJF.
Tel. 01793 741002

PYRENEAN MOUNTAIN DOG CLUB OF GREAT
BRITAIN, BS, CZ
Mrs L Ireland, The Gables Kennels, Garlands Lane,
Barlestone, Nr Nuneaton, Warwickshire CV13 OJD
Tel: 01530 230278. Email:
liz@lewiscedm.supanet.com. Web: www.pyre-
nean-sheepdog-club-of-gb.org

SAMOYED ASSOCIATION, BS
Miss A Haffenden, 6 Wetherby Gardens, Bletchley,
Milton Keynes, Bucks MK3 5NP.
Tel: 01908 379624

SAMOYED BREEDERS & OWNERS LEAGUE, BS
Mr J I Rees, 19 Richmond Crescent, Islington,
London N1 OLZ.
Tel: 0207 607 8971

ENGLISH SHETLAND SHEEPDOG CLUB, BS, TC, RC,
CZ, AG
Mrs J Johns, Silverbrink Cottage, Old Wood,
Skellingthorpe, Lincoln LN6 5UA.
Tel: 01522 509040

SCOTTISH SHETLAND SHEEPDOG CLUB, BS
Mr G Wyse, 2 Maryfield Gardens, Leslie,
Fife KY6 3JT.
Tel: 01592 744139

WELSH CORGI CLUB, BS
Mrs I Hughes, 1 Merlins Avenue, Merlins Bride,
Haverfordwest, Pembrokeshire SA61 1JS.
Tel: 01437 762292

⊕ Toy

AFFENPINSCHER CLUB, BS
Mrs A J Teasdale, Crabtree, Hamm Court,
Weybridge, Surrey KT13 8YE.
Tel: 01932 847679

BICHON FRISE CLUB OF GREAT BRITAIN, BS
Mr J Reynolds, 24 Cherington Close, Redditch,
Worcestershire B98 OBB.
Tel: 01527 517116. Email: secretary@bichon-
friseclubofgb.info. Web:
www.bichonfriseclubofgb.info

CAVALIER KING CHARLES SPANIEL CLUB, BS, AG
Mrs A Jones, The Old Swan, Carrog, Nr Corwen,
Denbigshire LL21 9AY.
Tel: 01490 430554

BRITISH CHIHUAHUA CLUB, BS
Mrs C Towler, 12 Peartree Close, Northumberland
Heath, Erith, Kent.
Tel: 01322 351961

LONGCOAT CHIHUAHUA CLUB, BS
Mrs S Lee, 3 Weir Vale Cottage, Old Burghclere,
Nr Newbury, Berks RG20 9NR.
Tel: 01635 278510

SMOOTHCOAT CHIHUAHUA CLUB, BS
Mrs D Grant, Woodend, Black Firs Lane, Marston
Green, Solihull B37 7JE.
Tel: 0121 782 4273

COTON DE TULEAR CLUB OF THE UNITED KING-
DOM (PROVISIONAL), BS
Ms H Gill, White Gable, Green Lane, Old Leake
Commonside, Boston, L.incs PE22 9QA.
Tel: 01205 871834

ENGLISH TOY TERRIER (BLACK & TAN) CLUB, BS
Mr N Gourley, Millstone Cottage, Derby Road, Nr
Osmaston, Ashbourne, Derbyshire DE6 1LZ.
Tel: 01335 300769

GRIFFON BRUXELLOIS CLUB, BS
Mrs M Oliver, 20 The Bridle Road, Purley, Surrey
CR8 3JA.
Tel: 020 8660 0969

ITALIAN GREYHOUND CLUB, BS, CZ
Dr R Phillips-Griffiths, 'Amberwood', Rhosgoch, Nr
Hay on Wye, Builth Wells. Powys LD2 31Y.
Tel: 01497 851649

KING CHARLES SPANIEL ASSOCIATION, BS
Mrs M Moss, Sombur, Wood Lane Small Dole,
Henfield, West Sussex BN5 9YF.
Tel: 01273 493582

KING CHARLES SPANIEL CLUB, BS
Mrs T Jackson, Amantra Kennels, Summers Lane,
Banwell, N Somerset BS24 6LR.
Tel: 01934 822758

MINIATURE PINSCHER CLUB, BS
Ms M Burns, 4 Natalia Terrace, Maiden Newton,
Nr Dorchester, Dorset DT2 0AR.
Tel: 01300 321293

PAPILLON (BUTTERFLY DOG) CLUB, BS
Mrs C Allward-Chebsey, 44 Gilbert Road, L.ichfield,
Staffordshire WS13 6AX.
Tel: 01543 256394

PEKINGESE CLUB, BS
Miss A Summers, 20 Tyrrell Square, Mitcham,
Surrey CR4 35D.
Tel: 020 8685 0371

PEKINGESE REFORM ASSOCIATION, BS
Miss V Williams, Berrylands Farm, Stanford,
Pirbright, Surrey GU24 0DG.
Tel: 01483 233377

POMERANIAN CLUB, BS
Mrs A Cawthera, Wheatley Gran;e,
Wheatleasowes Nr Telford Shropshire TF6 6DS.
Tel: 01952 604298

PUG DOG CLUB, BS
Mrs A Nicholson, 16 Chelsea Embankment,
London, SW3 4LA.
Tel: 020 7352 2436

YORKSHIRE TERRIER CLUB, BS
Mrs P E Mitchell, Mida, White Road, East Hendred
Oxon OX12
Tel: 01235 833171. Email:
pat@mida.freeserve.co.uk

ANIMAL WELFARE ASSOCIATIONS

These organisations may provide free treatment

RSPCA (Headquarters)
Wilberforce Way
Southwater
Horsham
West Sussex RH1 9RS
Tel: 0870 33 35 999
The RSPCA has forty branch-run clinics, thirty-seven animal centres, ten welfare centres. It rehomed over 96,000 animals in 2003. Contact their head office for more information

PDSA PetAid services
Freephone 0800 731 2502
A leading veterinary charity which treats more than 1 million cases per annum

The Blue Cross (Head Office)
Shilton Road
Burford
Oxon. OX18 4PF
Tel:01993 822651
Telephone their head office to find a branch near you

NATIONAL VETERINARY SCHOOLS

Royal (Dick) School of Veterinary Studies
Edinburgh

Faculty of Veterinary Science
University of Liverpool

Faculty of Veterinary Science
University of Cambridge

Royal Veterinary College
University of London

Faculty of Veterinary Medicine
University of Dublin

Faculty of Veterinary Medicine
University of Glasgow

School of Veterinary Science
University of Bristol

EMERGENCY VETS

Check your local phone book, or check with your local vet, to find out where your nearest one is, and keep the address and telephone number in a readily accessible place

PET- AND HOME-SITTERS

In theory, anyone can set up as a pet- or home-sitter, so make sure the one you choose is reliable and has good references. Try contacting:

The National Association of Registered Petsitters (NARP) Head Office
Tel: 01584 711534 Web: www.dogsit.com

All their members are registered and insured and they will be able to offer you a selection of their members in your region.

DOG CEMETERIES AND CREMATORIUMS

⊕ **South-east England**

Stephen and Susanna Mayles
The Cemetery and Cremantorium and Pets for Domestic Pets
Chestnut Lodge
Furnace Farm Road
Felbridge
East Grinsted
RH19 2PU

Clavenhambury Pet Cemetery & Crematorium
158 Chingford Mount Road
London
E4 9BS

Harry Hawkins
Chates Farm
Henfield Road
Cowford
Horsham
West Sussex
RH13 8DU

Happy Hunting Grounds
Little Park Farm
Hooe Road
Ninfield
Battle
East Sussex
TN33 9EH

Journeys End Pet Crematorium
Brissenden Green
Bethersen
Ashford
Kent
3N26 3JX

Sue Hemmings
Pets at Rest Cemetery & Crematorium
Pan Lane
Newport
Isle of Weight
PO30 2PJ

The Orchard Pet Cemetary
Basdell Park Farm
Crittenden Road
Matfield
Tonbridge
Kent
TN12 7EW

The Pets Country Crematorium
Longlane Farm
Long Lane
Shepherdswell
Dover
Kent
CT15 7LX

Sandhole Farm Pet Crematorium
Snodland Lane
Snodland
Kent
ME6 5LG

Vetspeed Ltd
A505 Main Road
Thripolow
Royston
Herts
SG8 7RR

Debbie Gilbert
Silvermere Haven Pet Cemetery
22 Clifton Road
Kingston-Upon-Thames
Surrey
KT2 6PH

Surrey Pet Cemetery & Crematorium
Byers Lane
South Godstone
Godstone
Surrey
RH9 8JL

Treasured Pets
Unit 8a Silkmead Farm Industrial Estate
Hare Street
Buntingford
Herts
SG1 0DX

Willow Haven
East Lane
Bedmond
Abbots Langley
Herts
WD5 0DQ

Trees Pet Cemetery
Copse Cottage
Hurst Lane
Sedlescoomb
Battle
East Sussex
TN33 0PE

Wymondley Pet Crematorium
Wymondley Bury
Little Wymondley
Hitchin
Herts
SG4 7JN

David and Monica Marshall
Aureole Pet Funeral Services
Tall Pines
Swansbrook Lane
Gunhill
Horam
East Sussex
TN21 0OL

⊕ Southern England

Kevin Spurgeon
Dignity Pet Crematorium
Brickfield
Odiham Road
Winchfield
Hook
Hants
RG27 8BU

Art Apart Memorial Plaques
12a Colville Road
Bournemouth
BH5 2AG

Island Pet Cemetery
North Fairlee Farm
Newport
Isle of Wight
PO30 3JU

Ginny Robson
Phoenix Pet Cremations
Blanford Road
Coombe Bissett
Salisbury
Wiltshire
SP5 4LN

Derek Bhowmik-Sherherd
Amberley Pet Cemetery
Woodmancote Lane
Hambrook
Chichester
West Sussex
PO18 8UL

⊕ South-west England

Companion's Rest
Phoenix House
Stoke Road
Elmstone Hardwicke
Cheltenham
Glos
GL51 9SY

Companion's Haven
Leighcroft
200 Westerleigh Road
Buckle Church
Bristol
BS16 3PY

Cremtor
Forches Cross
Newton Abbot
Devon
TO12 6PY

Lime Kiln Farm Companion Animal
Cremation Service
Lime Kiln Farm
Lypiatt
Stroud
Glos
GL6 7LP

Meadow Wood
Meadow Wood
Churchstow
Kingsbridge
Devon
TQ7 3QR

Petorium
Stonybridge
Pengover
Liskeard
Cornwall
PL14 3NH

John Lally
Penwith Pet Crematorium & Memorial Gardens
Rose Farm
Chyanhal Drift
Penzance
Cornwall
TN19 6AN

St Francis Pet Cemetery
Canaan House
Fiddlers Green
St Newlyn East
Newquay
Cornwall
TR8 5NL

Terry Squires
Terraine
Pontsmill
Par
Cornwall
PL24 2RR

⊕ Eastern England

Abbey Pets Remembrance Gardens
37 Salhouse Road
Rackheath Norwich
Norfolk
NR13 6PD

Cambridge Pet Crematorium
A505 Main Road
Thriplow
Royston
Herts
SG8 7RR

Abbey Pets Remembrance and Crematorium
Britons Lane
Bees Regis
Sheringham
Norfolk
NR26 8TP

Alton's Pet Cemetery
Arterial Road
North Benfleet
Wickford
Essex
SS12 9JG

Faithful Friends
White Lodge
London Road
Clacton on Sea
Essex
CO16 9RA

Ipswich Pet Cemetery
Cemetery Lodge
Toddenham Road
Ipswich
Suffolk
IP4 3QH

Lincolnshire Pet Crematorium
Woodbine Cottage
The Meeres
Kirton
Boston
Lincolnshire
PE20 1PR

Forget Me Not Animal Coffin Supplies
Westgate
Hunstanton
Norfolk
PE26 5EX

Norfolk Pet Cremation
Short Thorn Road
Felthore Road
Norwich
Norfolk
NR10 4DE

Orwell Pet Cremation Service
Stutton
Ipswich
Suffolk
IP9 2SX

Natures Meadows
Brome Avenue
Eye
Suffolk
IP23 7HW

Resting Pets Crematorium & Garden of
Remembrance
Wood Farm
Moreton Road
Ongar
Essex
CM5 0EY

Bill Phizackelia
Suffolk Pet Crematorium
Lower Farm
Great Saxham
Bury St Edmonds
Suffolk
IP29 5JT

⊕ Midlands

Animal Funeral Services Ltd
Barnes Hill
Birmingham
B29 5UP

Companion's Rest
Shinfield
Poffley End
Hailey
Witney
Oxfordshire
OX8 5UW

Buena Vista Pet Cemetery
Leicester Road
Frisby on the Wreake
Leicestershire
LE14 2PE

Green Pastures
Dove House
Hollington Lane
Stramshall
Uttoxeter
Stamfordshire
ST14 5EP

Lawnhill Farm
Eydon
Daventry
Northamptonshire
NN11 3PE

Longwood Pet Cemetery
PO Box 37
Walsall
West Midlands
WS1 2EF

Green Meadow Pet Caskets
Hartshill Road
Stoke on Trent
Staffordshire
ST4 6AB

Midland Counties Pet Crematorium & Memorial
Park
Brockall Park Road
Flore
Northampton
NN7 4LD

John and Rita Carlisle
Nottingham Pet Crematorium
Antara
Gamston Bridge
West Bridgeford
Nottingham
NG2 6NR

Pets at Rest
Burns Lodge
East Wall
Much Wenlock
Shropshire
TF13 6DU

Pet Cremation Service
West Lodge Farm
West Haddon Road
Guilsborough
Northampton
NN6 8QE

Pets Cremation Services Ltd
Bentley Moor Lane
Adwick-le-Street
Doncaster
DN6 7BD

Pet Heaven Ltd
36 Beech Walk
Dewsbury
West Yorkshire
WF13 2PJ

The Poffins Co
Poffins House
1 Walpole Close
Kings Meadow
Bicester
Oxon
OX26 2YF

The Blue Cross
Shilton Road
Burford
Oxon
OX18 4PF

PDSA
Whitechapel
Priorslee
Telford
Shropshire
TF2 9PQ

Derek Lawrence
Pet Crematorium
Prestwood Pet Crematorium
Stapenhill Farm
Prestwood Drive
Stourton
Nr Stourbridge
DY7 5QT

⊕ North-east England

Bushy Hill Pets Crematorium
Bushy Hill Farm
North Newbald
York
YO43 4TJ

Cleveland Pet Crematorium
Charlton Garage
Saltburn by the Sea
Cleveland
TS12 3AD

Chapel Moore Pet Crematorium
Brandesburton
Driffield
North Humberside
YO25 8EW

Richard Smith
Green Acres Pet Crematorium
Messingham Lane
East Butterwick
Nr Scunthorpe
South Humberside
DN17 3AS

Pets at Rest Cremation Service
Jerusalem Road
Half Acre Farm
Thornton
Bradford
West Yorkshire
BD13 3SG

The Pet Cremation
Willows
Langley Park Industrial Estate
Wittin Gilbert
Durham
Co. Durham
DH 6TX

Mr R Hodson-Walker
Badger Wood Pet Crematorium
Breach Farm
Caldwell
Derbyshire
DE12 6RJ

Honley Pet Crematorium
Clitheroe Farm
Scotgate Road
Honley
Huddersfield
West Yorkshire
HD7 2RE

⊕ North-west England

John Carlisle
The Association of Private Pet Cemeteries &
Crematoria
Nunclose
Armathwaite
Carlisle
CA4 9JT

Nick Ricketts
Paws to Rest Pet Bereavement Services
Coombs View
Nunclose
Armathwaite
Carlisle
Cumbria
CA4 9TJ

Leyland Pet Cemetery
Wigan Road
Leyland
Preston
Lancashire
PR5 2DA

Rossendale Pet Crematorium & Memorial Gardens
Crawshawbooth
Rossendale
Lancs
BB4 8UE

Tony Faulker
Whitley Brook Crematorium & Cemetery for Pets
Lady Hayes Farm
Kingsley Road
Frodsham
Cheshire
WA6 6SU

Hanover Memorial Gardens for Pets
1 Oakcroft
Stalybridge
Cheshire
SK15 2QU

The Pet Crematorium
Glazebrook Lane
Glazebrook
Warrington
Cheshire
WA3 5BL

⊕ Scotland

Elysian Fields Pets Cremations
Murdoch Place
Old Hall Industrial Estate
Irvine
Ayrshire
KA11 5DG

Elysian Fields Pets Cremations
9 Barr Terrace
Kirkmuirhill
Lanarkshire
ML11 9RQ

Hamilton (Irvine) Ltd
Murdoch Place
Oldhall Industrial Estate
Irvine
Ayrshire
KA11 5DG

Flatfield Garden of Rest
Errol
Perthshire
PH2 7RW

Ada Irving
The Pet Cremation
Unit 3, Block 2
Baird Avenue
Strutherhill Industrial Estate
Larkhill
Lanarkshire
ML9 2PJ

Michael M Strachan
Pets Crematorium
Wardhead Croft
Balmeadie
Aberdeen
AB23 8YJ

Leanne Fairbairn-Shaw
Abercorn Pet Bereavement Service
204 Piercefield Terrace
Portobello Road
Edinburgh
EH8 7BN

Pets Royale Funeral
4 Overdale Gardens
Glasgow
G42 9QQ

Craufurdland Pet Pasture
Midland Farm Cottage
Fenwick
Ayrshire
KA3 6BY

Pet Planet
10 Lindsay Square
Deans Industrial Estate
Livingston
Scotland
EH54 8RL

⊕ Wales

John Ward
Pet Funeral Services
Coetia Mawr
Brynford Hill
Brynford
Holywell
Clwyd
CH8 8AD

Summerleaze Pet Crematorium
Summerleaze Farm
Redwick
Magor
Newport
Gwent
NP6 3DE

Pets in Peace Pets Crematorium
Cwmdu Gandol Farm
Cwmdu
Maesteg
Mid Glamorgan
CF43 0DH

⊕ Northern Ireland

Robert Kelly
Cranmore Pet Crematorium
45 Tullyrusk Road
Dondrod
Crumlin
Co. Antrim
BT29 4JY

⊕ Channel Islands

Jayne Le Cras
Guernsey SPCA
Animal Shelter
Les Fiers Moutons
St Andrews
Guernsey
CIGY6 8UD

Ann Staite
Jersey SPCA
Animal Shelter
89 St Saviour's Road
St Hillier
Jersey
JE2 4LA

TAXIDERMISTS

The Guild of Taxidermy
c/o Glasgow Museums Resource Centre
200 Woodhead Road
Glasgow G53 7NN
Tel: 0141 276 9300

OTHER USEFUL ADDRESSES

Canine Lifeline UK
http://www.caninelifeline.co.uk
List of breed rescue clubs and associations. Dog rescue and training associations. Dogs needing homes. Help with dog problems.

The Cinnamon Trust (Head office)
10 Market Square
Hayle
Cornwall
TR27 4HE
www.cinnamon.org.uk

For an annual fee of £10 (£5 for OAPs) or a lifetime fee of £100, the Cinnamon Trust can find you a foster home (over 8,000 volunteers) for your dog, if you have to be hospitalised or can no longer cope through illness. And if you pre-decease your dog, they will find your dog a foster home, or care for it in one of their two sanctuaries in Cornwall and Devon.

Bibliography

There are a plethora of books on dogs on the market. Here are just a few useful ones:

Christopher Day, *The Homoeopathic Treatment of Small Animals*, The C.W. Daniel Co. Saffron Walden, 1984

Bruce Fogle, *The Dog's Mind: Understanding your Dog's Behaviour*, Howell Reference Books

James M. Giffin, Liisa Carlson *et al.*, *The Dog Owners Home Veterinary Handbook*, John Wiley, 1999

Kennel Club, *Year Book*, Kennel Club, 2004–5

Nico Maritz, *Your Sick Dog*, Swan Hill Press, Shrewsbury, 2004

David Sands, *Family Pet Guide: Dogs*, HarperCollins, 2002

Mike Stockman, *Dog Breeds of the World*, Lorenz Books, London, 1998

Uwe Streitfordt, Christine Metzger, Claus-Michael Pautzke, *Healthy Dog, Happy Dog: A Complete Guide to Dog Diseases and their Treatments*, Barron

JUL - - 2009

Lagalisse, Olivier.
How to make an old dog happy